FINDING YOUR POSTS
GROUNDED LIVING IN TIMES OF CHANGE

© Bar Sinister Publications

Names: Hickey, Kent

Title: Finding Your Posts: Grounded Living in Times of Change/ Kent Hickey

Subjects: Reflection. Spirituality. Personal Growth. Ignatian Spirituality. Spiritual Exercises. St. Ignatius Loyola. Humor. Catholic Education. Christianity. School Administration. Parenting. Graduation.

Printed in the USA. Nikko Media, Seattle, WA. March 15, 2017.

ISBN: 978-0-692-84811-1

To my loving family and dear friends.

Proceeds from Finding Your Posts *will be donated to support Seattle Nativity School, a Catholic, Jesuit middle school that seeks to "break the cycle of poverty through an education that nourishes souls and ignites leaders for love and service."*

CHAPTERS

ON...

LIVING SMALL DAYS..9

FINDING YOUR POSTS...13

GRAD TIDINGS...17

THE PLACES YOU WON'T GO 21

DISORDERED ATTACHMENTS.................................. 25

TECHNOLOGY... 31

EXERCISE 35

DISCERNMENT... 41

SPLITTING THE POSTS... 47

ABUNDANT LIVING 51

PARENTAL GUILT... 55

FORMATION 59

FRIENDSHIP... 63

DOGMATISM 67

GOODNESS... 71

MY TROPHY LIFE..75

GOD.. 79

MAKING MISTAKES 83

STAYING HUMAN 87

THE FRANCIS EFFECT...91

RAPTUROUS LIVING.. 95

JUDGING.. 99

FINDING MEANING IN VEGAS 103

LIFTING... 109

THE COLLEGE DROP OFF.. 113

FOREWORD

IN THE WORLD OF EDUCATION, there is a truism that in order to be a good teacher, one must also be a good learner. The same could be said of life: to live well one must be able to learn from life. Kent Hickey is an accomplished high school teacher and administrator, and he has also learned much from the connection between his life and his faith.

In fact, in my opinion, his ability to connect faith and life is exceptional, as is his ability to talk about their connection in insightful yet accessible ways. In these essays, Mr. Hickey shows us how his life and faith mutually enrich each other and does so in a refreshingly non-preachy way.

Mr. Hickey admits to being influenced by the spirituality of St. Ignatius of Loyola. Some say that Ignatius told his followers to "seek God in all things." Others say that he desired that they be able to "find God in all things." I believe that Mr. Hickey has done both.

As a friend of his for many years, I have always learned much from him. I think you will, too.

Frank Majka, SJ

INTRODUCTION

EVERY YEAR I talk to the freshman class on their first day of high school. Four years later, I talk to them at graduation. Those faces change, to be sure. But I'm always struck by how much their expressions on those two days are the same.

It's the eyes. Dazed, maybe even glazed, whether it be the first day of school or the last, the look is one of not knowing what they don't know, and kind of knowing that. Especially for the graduates, hazy thoughts about looming change swish around inside their heads while they fidget and sweat through speeches and awards. Foggy faces – that's what I see.

I also get a chance to look at parent faces at graduation. No fog in them, just a lot of quivering lips and watering eyes. They know that everything changes after graduation. It may come quickly with a child moving out or going to basic training within days after graduation. More often the change comes months later after the slow drip of summer gives way to the accelerated drama of the college drop off. But it's coming, and they know it. *Vita Mutatur.* Life changes.

And changes just keep coming. Work, military, college or grad school. Maybe a religious vocation. Marriage, or not. That first drive home from the hospital with a crying newborn in the backseat and the realization that this thing that's wailing away is never going away, a wonderful and scary epiphany.

Then it's career change, hopefully an individual choice but sometimes a forced one. Parents get older and the caregiver role turns upside down. Downsizing comes, retirement looms. Simple things taken for granted – like getting out of bed in the morning – get taxing.

Other things – like handling disappointments or being grateful for little things – get easier.

The only constant in all of this is change itself, and the anxiety, hope, sadness, joy, loss, or gain that comes with it. Transition – and especially being well positioned when it happens – is what this short collection of essays is about.

That being well positioned part is where *Finding Your Posts* comes in. I'm not sure how many times I've said that to goalkeepers in 30 years of coaching soccer, but I know it's been a lot. While a simple instruction, it's hard to keep in mind. As a game goes along, goalkeepers tend to look to the action as it moves away and their feet sometimes follow, causing them to drift from their goal posts. Keeping posts in mind keeps goalkeepers well positioned in front of their goal, allowing them to handle changes in play, especially when the action suddenly moves on top of them.

It is the same for all of us as we live our lives. Change comes, whether we want it to or not. If we're balanced and in good position in relationship to the goal, we can understand what is happening more easily and respond more readily. How we are living allows for better transitioning when that living changes.

I believe that we are never well balanced and ready for those changes when we are not in good relationship to the God-goal. These essays reflect that belief and are grounded in the balance that can be achieved through Ignatian spirituality.

"Ignatian" can be an intimidating word. It shouldn't be. It simply refers to the life, thoughts, and writings of St. Ignatius of Loyola, the founder of the Catholic order called the Society of Jesus (the Jesuits). While close to 500 years old, it's a spirituality that remains fresh and accessible. The best part of it, to me, is the basic belief that "God may be found in all things."

I take "all things" literally, meaning that God is accessible to us always and everywhere. In fact, boxing God into purely spiritual times and spaces boxes God out of the lives we actually lead. Looking for God in only the right places causes us to miss out on God in other places, and it's those other places that we often find ourselves living in.

These essays describe some not-so-right spaces to find God, places like a seedy workout gym and Vegas. As such, I'm going to admit that the content doesn't speak to piety in the customary sense. This book is more for those who, while not drawn so much to traditional spirituality books, are drawn to their center and see faith as a good way to keep from drifting. Consider this short compilation of essays, then, to be kind of like Seinfeld's "Festivus," a spirituality book for "the rest of us."

ON LIVING SMALL DAYS

IT'S NATURAL TO FOCUS on the big days in our lives – graduations, weddings, births. But, life itself is lived mostly in the small days in between big days. Further, how we live our lives in uneventful times flavors the eventful ones. The graduate who lives the days of four years really well, for example, really does have something to celebrate at graduation.

The same is true of a successful marriage, which has little to do with the wedding ceremony itself, as big as that day can be. And great parents arrive well before their babies do. It's the days leading up to the delivery room that tell us how exceptional parents will be, or not.

We live those small, in between days better when we stop and reflect at the end of each day. That's the Ignatian Examen, and that daily practice of examining one's day allows us to see the healthy and unhealthy patterns that continually shape our character – where we have responded with love to the events and people of the day, and where we have not.

They say that sports reveal character more than they build it. That's likely true. But, I think an even better revelation of character is commuting. At no time are our true selves revealed more than when we travel along with others, pilgrims on the journey of life, or maybe just to work or school. And each interaction along the way both reveals and shapes us, helping us to recognize the divine in others or, to borrow from Sartre, that "hell is other people."

My drive to work each morning is cut-throat, think *Lord of the Flies.* I escape by imagining myself riding through the Plains, the sun rising, dew hanging from thistles. It never works. I can't escape the fact that the sun is rarely seen rising in Seattle and that I don't even know what a thistle is. It's a feral commute, and each morning I gear up for battle.

Each morning I am also either fortunate or unfortunate enough to encounter along the way a small yellow bus with red lights flashing. The bus is picking up a special needs student and, since his mom always goes inside the bus with him, those red lights stay on for a long time and traffic gets backed up.

I am unfortunate when those red lights stay on and I am in a hurry and I am stuck there and I curse under my breath and feel pushed closer to the edge.

I am fortunate when those lights stay on and, even if I am in a hurry, I think about that mom taking care of her son so lovingly and feel blessed to witness such a beautiful, tender act.

The other day was a fortunate day. The mom once again took the youngster onto the bus while we all waited for those flashing red lights to turn off. For some reason, my eyes remained fixed on the dad standing on the sidewalk next to the bus. He just waved and waved to his son the whole time. I saw God in the gentle movement of a father's hand, opened to the son he loved.

After the red lights went off and the line started to move, the guy in the car in front of me honked his horn and flipped off the family. This bothered me when it happened, and it bothered me even more when, during my Examen that night, I recalled the number of times I flipped the same angry finger at that family in my heart.

Later that same week, the weather broke enough to invite me to ride my bike to work. From the start, things didn't go my way: My bike wasn't riding smoothly, and I hit every red light and pothole. I was even cut off by some guy wearing disturbingly small bike shorts. Is there such a thing as a bike thong? If so, shouldn't wearing one be a crime, even if just a crime against nature?

I was ticked and grousing under my breath at each perceived indignity and hardship. Then I came upon a group of riders who slowed me down, all of them wearing a t-shirt that read on the back, "Probably too old to be doing this." As I finally passed them I thought that this was likely true and prepared to flip a mental finger as I went by. Instead – to my surprise – I found myself smiling and waving. As I kept going, I also found myself in deep gratitude, the best kind of prayer of all.

When a day, big or small, lines up with a feeling of rightness, it's a blessing to just feel thanks. At those times I find myself in peace, recalling the times that day when I had built a little bit upon God's creation. "Thank you, God" becomes an easy prayer to say as I conclude my bedtime Examen.

After other, not so nurturing days, when I look at how my words and actions chipped away at the Kingdom and those I encountered, my prayer is a little different: "Please, God, help me to not be such a total ass tomorrow."

While the first prayer feels better to say than the second, they are both good prayers to say. Each helps me to see and live better the small days of my life, which are, after all, most days of my life. My hope is that when those big days arrive – especially that big one that awaits at the end of my days – there really will be something worth celebrating.

> *Here ends another day, during which I have had eyes, ears, hands and the great world around me. Tomorrow begins another day. Why am I allowed two?*
> -G.K. Chesterton

ON FINDING YOUR POSTS

FIND YOUR POSTS. That's one of the best lessons goalkeepers learn in soccer. Goalkeepers generally follow the action in front of them as opposed to being in the middle of it. As they watch they sometimes drift away from their goal. Drift too much and, when the action comes upon them, they are out of position. So, they must constantly remind themselves to find their posts so that they stay in proper relationship to the goal.

Ignatius Loyola, the founder of the Jesuits who lived about 500 years ago, lost sight of his posts as a young man. A lot. And, because he drifted so much, he sinned a lot too. While sin isn't used in soccer jargon, its original meaning should resonate with strikers: "to miss the mark." Ignatius missed the mark by huge margins and often.

Ignatius, for example, likely killed a man and then used a bogus religious protection to shield himself from prosecution. He viewed women as conquests. He pined for prestige. He was so vain that, when he saw a leg he had injured was healing in a way that wouldn't make him look hot in his tights, he corrected it with elective surgery (shaving off the bone without anesthetic). He drifted.

In his conversion, Ignatius found his posts. And when he found them and stayed near them, he also stopped missing the mark so much and certainly never missed so wide again. He did this by fixing his posts in a place that formed the center for his life: "Our goal is to be with God forever."

Ignatius called that primary goal, "The First Principle and Foundation." It serves as the basis for all Jesuit spirituality to this day and, since Ignatius formulated this spirituality primarily for laypeople while he himself was a layperson, it is accessible to all of us. That's why it's also referred to as Ignatian spirituality, so as to make clear it is not restricted to Jesuits.

Ignatius didn't become any less passionate after his conversion. He just re-directed his passion away from vanity, womanizing, and killing people to better passions. As a priest, for example, his love for the Eucharist caused him to shed tears so often and so much that his eyesight was diminished over time. Ignatius loved Jesus, and his most fervent prayer to God was that he be placed with His Son. However, at the same time, Ignatius was also highly rational and even rigid. His personality is reflected in the unique charism (defining characteristics) of the Jesuit order he founded. Both intensely passionate and systematic.

This apparent contradiction is reflected in the rest of the First Principle and Foundation. The opening assertion – "Our Goal is to live with God forever" – is aspirational and bold. But Ignatius followed the inspirational with instructions that sound like a "how to" manual: "We should not, therefore, fix our desires on health or sickness, wealth or poverty, success or failure, a long life or a short one."

This instruction forms the basis for what is now known as "Ignatian indifference." It is not indifference in the way our culture uses the word today (uncaring, ambivalent). Rather, it means that any desire needs to be considered in relation to the end that is sought. If it leads to it, good. If not, not so good. It's a way to find posts.

Further, Ignatius is clear that the end we seek – the God goal – is in the here and now, not a some day thing. So indifference needs to be practiced now, not down the line. That means being open to sickness, poverty, failure, and a short life – or to health, wealth, success and a long life – every day because on any given day one of those things may draw us closer to the goal of being closer to God or away from it.

Now, let me admit here that I just can't do that. I am not, for example, open to poverty because that would hurt my family and, frankly, I like my stuff. Sickness? Mrs. Hickey could describe how a severe cold draws parallels for me of Jesus on the cross, and how I then become a cross for her to bear. I can, and do, pray for greater indifference in my life so that I can keep my eyes on the prize (God). But that radical indifference Ignatius called for? I don't possess that kind of spiritual strength.

What I do possess, however, is a desire to find my posts. I get caught up with the action around me too easily, often finding myself far from goal in the most vulnerable times and spaces. I continue to be, much to my frustration, very much a work in progress, and I've concluded that I never will remain perfectly balanced and positioned. Still, the desire remains and I hope and pray that it stays with me. Thomas Merton, though not a Jesuit, captured a very Ignatian way of looking at all this:

"My Lord, I have no idea where I am going. I do not see the road ahead of me. Nor do I really know myself, and the fact that I think I am following your will does not mean I am actually doing so. But I believe the desire to please you does in fact please you. And I hope I have that desire in all that I am doing."

ON GRAD TIDINGS

I'VE LISTENED TO a lot of great graduation speeches in my lifetime. I just can't remember most of them.

I do recall one from many years ago that was given by a graduate who was better known for his humor than his study habits. He held up his official Hulk Hogan Growth Chart and, to very good effect, measured his uneven maturation against it. The other speech I remember, at my own college graduation, was given by none other than Captain Kangaroo. But all I recall is that we dropped ping pong balls when he was introduced. What I've concluded is that I only remember graduation speeches that include props.

It's not that I don't try to listen attentively to every word; it's just that random thoughts intrude. I've given out diplomas for close to 20 years, so, for example, during speeches I've found my thoughts drifting to how sweaty the handshakes will be and if I brought enough anti-bacterial lotion for afterwards. The thoughts that rumble through my head are generally not very deep thoughts.

I did, however, actually have a weightier thought at a recent graduation. It hit me that giving out special awards at graduation ceremonies is at best only a half-measure. Yes, recognizing past accomplishments is important; but, so too is aspiring for an award given at the other end of life. A full measure graduation ceremony, therefore, should include descriptions of awards that will be handed out at the graduates' 50th reunion. There should be two of them.

99% AWARD

THIS IS NOT the 99% on bumper stickers that separates 1% haves from 99% have-nots. Rather, this award is grounded in the following truth: It makes no sense and is a total waste of time to worry about what other people are thinking about us because – more than 99% of the time –they're not.

Though humbling, there is great freedom in knowing this. The theologian, Henri Nouwen, said that the two greatest threats to living life well are defining yourself by what you own and by what others think about you. I don't know which is worse, but knowing that others hardly ever think about us does remove a lot of anxiety.

Just saying this does not, of course, make it easy to live. That's why it's award-worthy. Parents take delight in how their young kids ask questions, share insights, and try new things without inhibitions. Teenage years change all that for most. Hands once readily raised in kindergarten become hesitant in high school. Clothing choices are made only after careful consideration of what others are wearing. Fear of failure replaces fearless adventure. And that tendency to define ourselves by what others think about us sticks around for a long time.

When we get much, much older it is easy to follow the 99% rule. Life teaches that being defined by the opinions of others is just stupid and, as those others die off over the years, it becomes a lot easier to not listen to them. The 99% Award is won, therefore, between the years after graduation and before senility sets in. That's why the 50 year reunion is the best time to give it.

COLIGE ROSAS AWARD

FOR 10 YEARS I was blessed with the gift of driving our kids to school each day. When I drove in with the oldest, our daughter, we parked in the bottom level of the building and walked up the stairs together. She would get off on the third floor and walk outside through the rose garden. I walked up to the fourth floor and, before going to my office, would pause to look out the window at the rose garden below as she walked through it.

Every day was the same – rain, shine or running late for first bell. She would stop at a rose bush, gently cup a rose in her hands and then breathe from it. I loved starting my day watching that.

An early Jesuit, Jerome Nadal, described the purposeful life as living "with one foot in the air." I like that image. It harkens to the kind of "go get 'em" advice often heard at graduations. Be more so that you can do more. Make a difference. Be the change you want to see in the world.

But every year a few weeks after graduation, I'm reminded that always holding one foot in the air can also lead to an imbalanced life. I attend a luncheon with our Golden Panthers, graduates of 50 years or more. Closer to the finish line than they are to the starting gate, their later in life transitioning pulls them closer to what is most dear to them. And awards simply don't make that list. It's all about how they've lived and how much they care for those with whom they've lived.

Those older grads would have simple advice for their younger counterparts: Drop that foot out of the air every once in a while, plant both feet on the ground, and stop at that rose bush. Colige Rosas. Gather ye roses, while ye may.

ON THE PLACES YOU WON'T GO

THERE'S A REASON why the Dr. Seuss classic, *Oh, the Places You'll Go* is such a popular graduation gift. It's the story of a kid who soars in a hot air balloon, much like the soaring hopes and dreams of graduates. A life of possibilities awaits, and even the sky doesn't have limits.

That's true, but not the whole truth, which is why the wise Dr. Seuss also describes the deflated times when the balloon is grounded. I think those times are the most telling ones in the story, a not-so-fun thought perhaps better not spoken aloud at graduation parties. Take another look at that book, though. Graduates garner inspiration enough from graduation itself. Dr. Seuss asks them to instead ponder what life is like when the high flying balloon is grounded and its occupant is stuck in the worst place of all, the waiting room.

It is certainly true that the high school graduate soars into college and then soars even higher while there. What later emerges with that college degree in hand bursts upon the world, ready to grasp hold and bend it to her will. Except that's not what happens, at least not right away. Waiting time often awaits. But waiting time is not wasted time, if the waiting time is done right.

I remember meeting with a recent college grad who had moved to Seattle. He wanted to talk about his career goal, a job at Starbucks that would involve traveling to Central America to educate coffee growers about sustainable farming practices. As we talked, it became clear that he knew little Spanish, even less about farming, and nothing about coffee, such as how to brew it. "Let's maybe start there," I suggested, "perhaps by becoming a barista. Learn the job from the grounds up." Advice which, I'm sure, deflated his balloon and plopped him into a waiting room.

I suggested that to him because, as I look back, I have been fortunate to have been stuck in some formative waiting rooms in my life, places where I learned more than I would have if I'd always been flying high.

For example, one of the worst and best jobs I ever had was driving an ice cream truck in a very rough Milwaukee neighborhood. My truck was rusted out and the music machine was broken, so I had to constantly ring a door bell on the dashboard instead. Low man in the organizational hierarchy, I had a high poverty route that was a little scary at times. But the customers I met seemed to take pity on me and were consistently pleasant. I didn't make much money, but I learned a lot about people and myself driving that route.

I found myself in another waiting room during law school. While most of my classmates clerked at high flying law firms with big names and paychecks, I ended up as a clerk at a small firm in a not-so-upscale part of Milwaukee. It was headed up by a former Chicago Cardinal football player who was said to have been an arms supplier for Serbian fighters and who hit me hard on the shoulder every time he thought I didn't love Jesus enough. Fortunately, however, another attorney was a wonderful mentor who gave me a lot of work that would never have happened at the big firms.

Ever wonder, for example, who incorporated "Bunkbed City and Mattress World" in South Milwaukee? Look no more. I was even the process server for the firm. I recall the day I served legal papers on the owner of a local candy shop. How hard could it be to serve the candyman – "Who can make the sunshine, turn the world around?" This particular candyman, however, was 300 lbs. and, once served, pulled out a baseball bat, somehow managed to jump over the counter, and chased me down the street. But I escaped. Eat it, candyman.

I waited when I practiced law too, this time at a small firm in Janesville, Wisconsin, "the land that time forgot." I became the name change master of Rock County, once even successfully petitioning a court to change a client's name from "James" to "Jimmy." Mostly I did probate and bankruptcy, so at a young age I had near daily interactions with people experiencing enormous heartache, loss, and stress. I learned the law, but it was those people who taught me the most.

The waiting room, when done well, prepares us for more active spaces and even soaring to all those places in that balloon Dr. Seuss described so beautifully. Still, the waiting room is often frustrating and can even feel empty and meaningless. The way through this is to concentrate on how to live there and not so much the muzak that's playing or the three-year-old People magazines lying on the table. That's why my favorite waiting room story is about a doorman.

Alphonsus Rodriguez lived hundreds of years ago, a man of means and proud head of his household. That is, until he lost his wife and his children. He listened for God's call and eventually found himself as a Jesuit, Brother Rodriguez. Since he had soared some in his life and had talents, Rodriguez held an expectation that his superiors would place him in a position of responsibility. They did. He was responsible for the door, as in opening it when someone rang the bell.

As Rodriguez waited for bells, he made a decision that changed his life: each time he greeted someone at the door, he would look for the face of Christ in that person. Bell rings, "Coming Lord," he would say. What happened over time was that he didn't need to pretend to see Christ's face – he simply did. The love that poured forth at every ringing of the bell was really the opening of a heart, and Brother Rodriguez, later Blessed Rodriguez, became a path to God through his door. It was all in the how, not the what.

There's a similar lesson in the movie, *Mr. Holland's Opus*. Holland wanted to be a great musician and write hit music. He didn't accomplish either goal. As he moved toward the end of his career he came to realize that his greatest opus – work – could be found in the faces of all those band kids he had taught in high school over the decades. That's not the place he wanted to go when he started out, but he was so happy that his balloon had carried him there.

None of this is to say we shouldn't strive to fly high in those balloons so that we can land in fantastic places. Seeking and striving are what we are made for. But how-we-go is at least as important as where-we-go, and sometimes living well in the waiting room is the best ticket.

> *You'll get mixed up, of course, as you already know. You'll get mixed up with many strange birds as you go. So be sure when you step, step with care and great tact. And remember that Life's a Great Balancing Act.*
>
> -Dr. Seuss, from *Oh, the Places You'll Go*

ON DISORDERED ATTACHMENTS

A FRIEND OF MINE tried to block his license plate when he noticed I was about to take a picture of it. This friend – severely limited by his sloth-like reflexes – was unsuccessful. What he has been very successful at is business judgment. He has earned great success and, because he is a generous person, has generously supported people and causes in need.

What to think, then, about the AMDG license plate on a Maserati? That's *Ad Majorem Dei Gloriam* – "for the greater glory of God" – the motto of the Society of Jesus (the Jesuits). Doesn't the Maserati brand conflict with that Jesuit brand? Perhaps. Does that mean that what the Maserati represents in my friend's life conflicts with what AMDG should represent to him? Maybe. Maybe not. It depends.

Ever hear of thirty-one year old Natasha Harris of New Zealand? She died of a heart attack, a strange thing for one so young and in most ways very healthy. Even stranger was the coroner's ruling on her cause of death: Too much soda. How much is too much? Ms. Harris drank two gallons of Coke a day.

I doubt that Ms. Harris awoke one morning with the thought, "You know what would be a really good idea? Drinking two gallons of Coke every day!" She probably started with a can or two – no problem – but drifted into over-consumption over time.

That story captures what St. Ignatius of Loyola, the founder of the Jesuits, called "disordered attachments." Ignatius, a man of the 16th century, was ahead of his time in the way he fused what we would today categorize as psychological maladies with spiritual ones.

To Ignatius, life was all about interior freedom, becoming the kind of human God had in mind when God created each of us. He noticed in his own life a tendency to abrogate his own freedom through the unhealthy choices he made. A long recovery from a war wound brought him to an understanding that his choices were often the result of unhealthy, even destructive, desires. So began a lifetime of reflection about the difference between good, healthy attachments and those that were not.

For Ignatius, that lifetime of reflection was all about the Examen, the practice of examining the movements of one's life within the day. It's simple to do but only works when done consistently: A few times a day, and especially at the end of the day, honestly review the thoughts, interactions, and events of the day. Over time a pattern may emerge – behaviors and decisions that feel false and are often destructive.

This simple, daily reflection is designed to help us recognize our unhealthy (disordered) attachments so that we can nurture healthier, more life-giving (ordered) attachments. St. Ignatius believed the source of any disordered attachment was a desire for riches, honors, or pride. (That is what the story of Jesus' temptation in the desert is really all about.) Of these, it appears that riches – becoming overly attached to possessions – pose the greatest danger. "It is harder for a rich man to enter heaven than for a camel to pass through the eye of the needle," warned Jesus. Or, if you prefer Brad Pitt from Fight Club, "The things you own end up owning you."

But wealth in and of itself need not lead to a disordered life. It could be that one's possessions are held in perspective and folded within a well-balanced, healthy life. Then again, it could also be that the desire for possessions devolves into an imperceptible, unhealthy slide toward selfishness and falseness.

We have on one hand, for example, the take of the wealthy socialite, Gloria Vanderbilt: "Anyone who doesn't believe that money can buy happiness doesn't know where to shop."

But we also have, on the other hand, a different take on shopping as described in a simple story from the Civil War. Two Union generals, Kearney and Howard, had been best friends since their service in the Mexican War years earlier. Kearney had lost his left arm in the Mexican War and later, in the Civil War, Howard lost his right arm. Kearney visited his friend in the hospital where he reassured him, "From hereafter, we will buy our gloves together."

Both stories are about shopping and not about shopping. Mrs. Vanderbilt's attachment to stuff reflects arrogance and disregard for the poor. General Kearney's attachment is to something quite different. Shopping for gloves plays a bit part in the bigger story of the desire to comfort a friend in need.

But here's the thing lest we become too focused on riches – the attachment that knocks us off track and messes up our lives can be anything. So, to decide if an attachment is healthy or unhealthy, ordered or disordered, look more to what it does than what it is. Use of alcohol, for example, isn't the same as addiction to it. The alcohol itself isn't the problem; addiction to it is.

My college roommates all played rugby, and I recall watching a very large freshman at one of their games. He played on the top team and moved with an agility and grace that belied his size. I went to their party after the game and was introduced to the freshman, named "Pig." Already drunk, only half of his body was covered. The top half. I remember shaking his hand very carefully.

That freshman was Chris Farley, who after graduation starred at Second City in Chicago and then went on to fame on *Saturday Night Live* and in movies. But he almost didn't make it out of college. His addiction to alcohol, even as a freshman, brought him to a dismissal board. But a Jesuit saved him, calling Farley a tireless worker on behalf of the poor and a daily communicant. That's right – Chris Farley went to Mass every day. Farley ended up dying of an overdose, his disordered attachments overwhelming a life full of goodness and promise.

There are so many other ways that lead into unhealthy attachments in college, and in life. Getting good grades is one. Hard work that pays off in the reward of a good grade is generally a healthy and good thing. But what if the grade replaces learning as the ultimate goal and that desire trumps character? Caving into the temptation to cheat once makes it easier the next time, and then more times thereafter, so that one discretion becomes a pattern and a person who once cheated becomes a cheater. Two gallons of Coke a day.

Let's go back to Jesus' warning about how difficult it is for a camel to pass through the eye of the needle. That "eye of the needle" was an actual gate, a very narrow one, into Jerusalem. Camels had to be unloaded before they could squeeze through. It is the same thing with unhealthy attachments: we don't get to where we want to go while overloaded with baggage. And that burden, like the links in the chain of Marley's ghost, is built up, often imperceptibly, over time.

Let's also go back to the picture of my friend's car. If what is central to that shot is "Maserati" and if that is keeping him out of Jerusalem, it's got to be unloaded. If, however, the key to that car is the AMDG license plate and the Maserati could just as easily be replaced by "Jetta" or even "Pinto," then that's a whole different take. Either way, the disordered or ordered attachment question is one only the individual person can answer.

> *There have been some who were so occupied in spreading Christianity that they never gave a thought to Christ…Did ye never know a lover of books that with all his first editions and signed copies had lost the power to read them? Or an organizer of charities that had lost all love for the poor? It is the subtlest of all the snares.*
>
> – C.S. Lewis, from *The Great Divorce*

ON TECHNOLOGY

THESE AMAZING PICTURES capture *"habemus papam"* moments at St. Peter's Square: 2005 for Pope Benedict and 2013 for Pope Francis. What a change in only eight years. The next time there is a "We have a Pope" event at St. Peter's Square there will likely be even more gadgets waving in the air. Technology continues to transform how we live – and how we live with each other – in good and not so good ways.

I recall an op-ed piece written by a perceptive young waitress that alluded to a Thoreau quotation, "Men have become tools to their tools." She described how dining has changed in recent years, what with the prevalence of customers eating in silence, hunkered down at tables while consuming their cellphones.

In Seattle that kind of behavior is now common on city sidewalks crowded with Microsofties, Googlers, and Amazonians. I've been to college commencement ceremonies where graduates are more immersed in their phones than their graduation. Texting while driving now causes as many accidents as drunk driving, and texting during conversations is just taken as a given, as if it's a natural (and polite) thing to do.

But it is not technology itself that is the problem. Hard to blame tools if we have allowed ourselves to become their tools.

A few years ago I had the privilege of serving as host to Jim Sinegal, founder of Costco, for a presentation and question/answer session with students. One senior asked why it was that Costco was known for treating its employees so well while Walmart had a very different reputation. Mr. Sinegal said it was all about culture, what was valued and what was not.

As I walked with Mr. Sinegal to his car after the session (secretly hoping to score some free hot dog coupons), I complimented him on his answer and asked a follow up question: "Are you concerned about Costco becoming more like Walmart as leadership transitions to new generations?" Mr. Sinegal explained that creating culture is very difficult, but once firmly rooted (for good or bad) it is hard to reshape. He believed that Costco's culture would remain true to its principles because its roots ran so deep.

We may now be a hopelessly entrenched "tools of our tools" culture. On the other hand, however, maybe recent trends in our use of technology are not so deeply rooted and we could grow in a healthier direction. How can we tell? Count the cars. There is a farmer in the Midwest who predicts recessions based upon fluctuations in the number of railcars that pass by his property. Perhaps counting cars applies to culture as well as economics.

If so, there are signs that the technology pendulum is swinging back toward less obsessive and more humane use. More friends are establishing no cellphone rules when out for dinner. More parents are requiring that cellphones be put in a kitchen basket during study time and are charged at night outside bedrooms. Some millennials, hoping to focus on the agenda during meetings, are limiting their tools to spiral notebooks and pens to decrease distractions. Those high schools that didn't cave into unlimited student use of cellphones are now the envy of those that did. And Amazonians who insist on burying their heads in their cellphones while on Seattle sidewalks are now openly mocked. (Not a nice thing, but a kind of satisfying one.)

The deeply rooted hunger for companionship likely runs deeper than the dopamine that is released with constant texting. Our culture could reflect this truth once again. But that will take a commitment to put people before tools.

ON EXERCISE

THE THINK TANK at Fitbit must have believed us all to be gullible suckers if they thought that the buzz on a wristband when 10,000 steps are reached in a day could actually incentivize lazy people. Well, count me as a gullible sucker. When I hit 10k on a day I let everyone around me, including strangers, know it.

I need all the help I can get. It's been so easy for me to drift into sedentary living. I think it started in college. What I gained from inactivity was the Freshman 15. What I lost was opportunities for stress reduction, developing a pattern of healthy exercise, and perhaps even brain volume. That's right. Studies have shown that regular exercise, especially aerobic workouts that increase heart rate and get sweat glands pumping, actually increases brain volume. This includes the hippocampus, the learning part of the brain.

That commitment to regular exercise makes even more sense to me now, what with additional concerns about high cholesterol and the possible link between strength/fitness and warding off early signs of dementia. I've also found that working out helps me to think things through better when I have a problem and gives me a greater sense of peace, even tranquility. Conversely, when I go a stretch without working out, I feel more out of sorts and on edge. So, there are many reasons why committing to strength/fitness health make sense.

Just because something makes logical sense, however, isn't enough to get me doing it. I need more. Getting my Fitbit has helped. So also has joining a fitness center, though it certainly isn't a fancy one. Located on a street where it is the last business not hawking cheap liquor, pedaling marijuana, or featuring pole dancers, it's a lowly place for the low brow. But I go anyway, while making sure that I always spray down equipment and never sit on toilet seats. Truth is I fit right in with the less-than-beautiful people.

But what really gets me off the couch and going is music. I love listening to music and have created a truly awesome playlist. I allow myself to listen to it only while working out. In addition to incentivizing me to exercise regularly, it has also allowed me to match music with each work out phase, thus elevating the quality of my workout while increasing my enjoyment. Is my playlist perfect for workouts and the best that has ever been made? Yes.

Stage 1 of my workout consists of highly personalized yoga postures, such as "Extended Arm Toward Fluorescent Lights." Reflective music matches the mood: Pink Floyd, Natalie Merchant, and James Taylor.

I must be careful, however, during the tranquil music /yoga stage that I not be absorbed into songs of regret and angst, lest I become trapped in workout stupor. Here I have foolishly allowed myself to be pulled into a Jackson Browne dirge with its soul crushing lyrics, "And the fear of living for nothing strangles your will." This yoga posture is entitled, "Fetal Position."

I feel the burn, and a little more sweat, in Stage 2: Low weights/low repetition. My heart rate is jumpstarted by heart pounding music: Leonard Cohen's *The Future*, Nirvana's *Smells Like Teen Spirit,* and Peter Gabriel's *Big Time.*

Stage 3 – elliptical training – provides a brief pause for a mid-day Ignatian Examen. I keep it simple. "Help me, Lord, to see those times this day when I responded with love to your loving presence in my life, and those times when I did not." If the Examen leaves me feeling gratitude and peace, I move right back to my workout playlist. If not, AC/DC's *Highway to Hell* and *Panic Switch* by Silversun Pickups remind me to ramp up my efforts.

I can feel my expanding hippocampus pressing against my skull. Can't waste it. Time to take a break and resolve a couple of questions that have been vexing me. Awesome anniversary gift for my wife? Check. Home Depot gift card. What inspirational quote to put on this year's t-shirts for the girls' soccer team I coach? Eminem's *Lose Yourself* provides the answer. No, not "You've only got one shot." Too obvious. I'm going with, "There's vomit on his sweater already. Mom's spaghetti." The players – and their parents – will love it!

For some reason the machines near me go unused even during the busiest times. No matter to me. Here some sweat in my eyes – and definitely not tears – has caused a brief pause in my workout during the (dearly departed) Clarence Clemons sax solo in Springsteen's *Jungleland.*

I sometimes wonder why our Board of Trustees requires me to wear t-shirts from rival schools when I exercise in public. But I'm too zoned in to worry about that. Time to ellipticate to the finish while listening to guilty pleasures like *Drops of Jupiter, Personal Jesus,* and *Get Down Tonight.* So ends the most grueling workout this side of hell.

ON DISCERNMENT

I TEAM-TEACH a senior seminar about human nature. We spend a lot of time on philosophy, much of it centered on what constitutes a meaningful life. We take those ancient Greeks at their word that the end we seek is happiness. But how do we get there?

That's where discernment comes in. We make decisions all the time: "Why, yes, I will have another beer. Nachos too? Absolutely." Small choices can sometimes add up and lead to the necessity to make bigger decisions: "Wonder if I should make some lifestyle changes so I can drop those 20 lbs. I've inexplicably gained this year?"

But most of our daily choices don't call for discernment. It's for the really big stuff, questions about the right path to take in life and the right thing to do when faced with perplexing questions.

I once asked a Jesuit Provincial if I should wade into a particularly vexing question. "Engage the gray," he told me. The gray is any question that is layered with competing principles, sound arguments on both sides and laden with emotion. Avoid-and-hope-it-goes-away is one way to deal with the gray, but is, of course, the wrong way. Better instead to address it through a process of discernment.

Discernment is a special kind of prayer. Instead of making an important decision on my own, I instead choose to walk with God in making that decision. I wrote a note, for example, to our youngest son as he was considering what college to attend and asked him to place it on his nightstand: "Give me, Lord, the wisdom to know your will and the courage to follow it." Yes, there are steps to good discernment, but the journey begins, continues, and ends always with God.

While there is no set pattern to good discernment, a really good place to start is reflection, sitting with the question and noodling on it. Frame reflection around freedom. What are the factors that are limiting my freedom to make the right decision? Maybe those limitations come from within. I may have fallen into an unhealthy, disordered attachment that is carrying more influence than it should. I, for example, am a driven person, a good thing when in balance, but not so good when taken too far. That desire to get things done can overwhelm other desires that should be in play.

It's also important to recognize the limitations from without – relationships that should be considered and pressures to shape the decision one way or another. The intentions of those trying to exert influence should be given weight, remaining mindful that the intentions of some may be more self-serving than in the service of the common good.

While reflecting upon these factors it is also important to honestly admit to myself what I am afraid of. I could be fearful, for example, of hurting someone I am close to or having to make a sacrifice I don't want to make. Fear diminishes discernment. Acknowledging fear may not eliminate it, but will reduce its impact.

Those steps – reflection about healthy and unhealthy attachments, recognizing outside influences, and acknowledging fear – help move us into a position of greater interior freedom that elevates the desire to do the right thing above the desire to do other things. And that desire to do right generally leads to actually doing it. Sounds simple, but it's not. That other stuff that gets in the way is often very attractive stuff.

Some years ago I was faced with a decision about what to do about a graduate of our school, Amanda Knox. Amanda had been charged with the murder of her roommate in Perugia, Italy and was being held in jail awaiting trial. Amanda was innocent but at the time this wasn't known. Reporters from around the world were covering the case and it became a media sensation. Camps of passionate opinion holders were quickly formed.

As I pondered what would be the right thing to do, a fearful voice inside me insisted that doing nothing would be a really good idea. This approach would have been in keeping with a maxim from *A Man for All Seasons* that often makes sense to me, "Whatever may be accomplished by smiling, you may rely upon me to do."

But entering the question in a spirit of discernment – including conversations with people more courageous than myself and a lot of "give me the wisdom to know your will and courage to follow it" prayer

– eventually led me to the conclusion that we should support Amanda. And so we did, with letters, care packages, and fundraisers for her family's legal defense fund. Then came the firestorm: negative media, hateful emails, withdrawn financial support for the school and attacks by some influential people.

Strangely, though, none of those things bothered me. The decision just felt right, then as now, and a kind of peace settled within me. Before the decision, while weighed down by an unhealthy attachment to self-preservation and very fearful, the prospects of such negativity and conflict filled me with anxiety. Discernment, though, requires seeing with clear eyes, detached from desires that blur the distinction between the right thing to do and the expedient one. "The truth will set you free," it's been said. That same freedom comes from acting upon the desire to do the right thing, and with that freedom comes peace.

The characteristics of good discernment also apply to questions about one's direction in life – college or no college; which college; this job or that; marriage and if so to whom; kids and, if so, how many. But this kind of question is more personal, so more is needed. That something more is gratitude, a profound appreciation for the gifts both within and around us. From these gifts, and our gratitude for them, we see possibilities, especially the possibility of happiness.

A wise Jesuit once told me that happiness is not just something I desire for myself. It is also something God desires for me. That's what is meant by finding and following God's will – the center of discernment when making big decisions about life. Sometimes this desire to follow God's will is mischaracterized as a kind of interior enslavement, a negated freedom found in a sacrificed life. Not so. Finding and doing what God desires for us is actually a journey into freedom and fullness of life because who I really am can't be distinguished from the person God is calling me to be.

I keep a resignation letter from a teacher near me at my desk. I keep it there because her words remind me of what good discernment looks like: "This school is a fantastic place; yet, I am constantly confronted by what James Martin, SJ calls '[being] who you is.' When I reflect on who I am, it is in living and working with the poor in Latin America that I truly come alive. That is where my heart's deepest desire is met and it brings out the best in me, so I must go!"

That simple letter captures it all, including that last line that points to the final step in good discernment: "so I must go!" Hands follow the heart. Living the fruit of good discernment does not make for easy living, but it does make for right living. Ultimately, as my Jesuit friend told me, we find that what we want for ourselves – and what God wants for us – is the same thing: Happiness.

ON SPLITTING THE POSTS

I'VE NOTICED over my years in high school administration that when a parent has a complaint about athletics it's almost always about playing time (even if it's dressed up to look like something else). I get it. It's more fun playing than not playing, and to watch your child sitting on the bench can be hard. The truth in life, however, is that almost all of us reach a stage where we look around and see that we're just not as good as the competition. That realization often hits in high school.

I was a lineman on my high school football team and lost what I thought was my starting position early in senior year. I never spoke with my parents about my demotion, probably because I was embarrassed and uncomfortable. Years later, though, I asked my mom if she or my dad had ever done what I've seen other parents do – complain to the coach. "No, we didn't," she said. "We had a lot of things going on and also, honey, you just weren't very good."

Luckily for me I played football at a different position too – kicker. To which the reader may now think, "Well, then you really didn't play football." I loved it, though. Those times when I struck a ball just right felt so pure. Over the years I've enjoyed coaching kicking and still occasionally take a football out and kick some extra points. It's a lot of fun.

But kicking in high school games when it mattered wasn't that fun for me. I worried too much, which is not a good thing for kickers to do. Rather than clearing my mind and just trying to strike the ball with good form, I sometimes feared missing. At those times I kicked timidly and without follow through. Instead of splitting the posts I would hook left or shank right.

I wish I could have been more of the mind of the legendary hockey player Wayne Gretzky: "You miss every shot you don't take." I like that confidence and gusto. But sometimes in kicking – and now I am not really talking about kicking – I've noticed that I've been at my worst when I feared what would happen if I did take a shot. Thoughtfulness and caution are good things; over-thinking and paralysis are not.

Knowing that fear of failure often froze me in high school – so I didn't try out for that play, or ask that girl out, or got the yips while kicking – is probably a big reason why I talk about the *magis* so much while working with young people today. The *magis* is Latin for "the more" and it's an essential value in Jesuit education: Be more so that you can do more.

I use *magis* and not "excellence" as the standard because I think excellence is a results word. That is, excellence is about top 10 lists, championships and judging from without. The *magis* is a within word, as in the interior awareness of knowing the difference between trying one's best and not. Results are generally outside our control. Effort isn't.

Seeking the *magis* – how hard we try and how much we strive – falls fully within our purview. The happy outcome that often comes with seeking the *magis* (inside) is that we are then often rewarded with an excellent result (outside). If, however, seeking the result replaces effort as the goal then the goal is misplaced. In other words, we need to embrace the possibility of ending up with less when we seek more.

Which brings me back to kicking in high school. I remember well a big game we had against our biggest rivals. It was Monsignor Hackett (us) against Kalamazoo Christian (them). Catholics vs. Lutherans. Papists vs. Heretics.

We scored a touchdown and I went out to kick the extra point. I was blessed with a feeling of total confidence, locked into the moment despite the crowd, noise and tension. Perfect hike, perfect hold, and perfect kick. Dead center – into the stomach of a lineman who came up the middle completely unblocked. I scooped up the ball from the ground and ran as fast as I could, and was then tackled by the other 10 players. The back of my uniform covered in mud – a humiliating symbol akin to being shot in the back in battle – I trotted off the field to the sidelines.

Did I mention that we lost the game, 7-6? In the newspaper the next morning was the damning box score line, "kick failed." But, as hard as that failure was to take, I felt good about my honest effort. I didn't miss that kick – I just happened to hit a stomach. While at other times I had caved into a fear of failure, in that particular moment I hadn't and had given it my best shot. I'd never heard of the *magis* at that time, but that's what I had been seeking.

I've missed splitting the posts a lot in life. The only times I regret, however, are the ones when I hadn't given my best shot. Missing when striking well isn't a failure, even if by all outward appearances it appears to be.

ON ABUNDANT LIVING

A FEW YEARS AGO I saw a bumper sticker on an old, beat up pickup truck: "I always wanted to be somebody. Guess I should have been more specific."

We should all want to be somebody. It's a good thing to strive for exceptionalism. Nelson Mandela once quoted a poet as he exhorted his countrymen to reach high: "You are a child of God. Your playing small doesn't serve the world." We can play big while playing humbly. We can climb to the top without climbing over the bodies we've slain to get there. Being good and being great are not mutually exclusive.

But none of that balancing matters if we do not first possess the belief that we can indeed journey to the heights. Exceptionalism requires hope.

A philosophical movement emerged after World War II called Existentialism, so called because the foundation of its philosophy was that we exist first and then create who we are, our essence, in the decisions we make throughout our lives. Existentialists hold as a basic truth that we are all free to make the selves we want to be.

But that basic understanding led different Existentialists down different paths, and the pivot point was hope, or not. Some, while wearing black and sipping coffee in Parisian cafes, wrote about the condemnation of freedom in uplifting books like, "Being and Nothingness." Instead of seeing possibilities in relationships, they asserted that "hell is other people." The awesome responsibility of freedom overwhelmed them with ennui (boredom), angst, despair, and the only real question they thought was worth asking, "Why not commit suicide?"

Other Existentialists, while accepting that freedom could create a responsibility that becomes burdensome, took a much different approach. They pivoted on hope, determined to find meaning and purpose in life, even if life appeared bereft of meaning and purpose. So, for example, in *The Plague*, Camus wrote about a doctor who continues to treat patients suffering from an illness that has no cure. Similarly, Camus turned a hopeless tale – *The Myth of Sysiphus* – on its head. In the Greek myth, Sysiphus is condemned by the gods to eternal futility: He must roll a rock up a hill, only to have it tumble back down, each time for all time. But Camus didn't leave Sysiphus without hope. Instead, as that rock rolls back down the hill, Sysiphus looks to it with determination and even happiness, taking hope from a most hopeless situation.

How much or how little hopefulness we possess may be tied to our nature, but it certainly also depends upon how we are nurtured. Young people are especially vulnerable to the sounds of "can't" and "just settle for." And it's our schools that often set that low bar.

I recall stopping at a red light on a busy street near a large high school. On the corner was the school reader board, a place for the school to provide information or inspiration. It must have been inspiration day because the sign read, "Go to class. Be nice." I asked our teenage son sitting next to me what he thought the sign meant. He answered, "Isn't that kind of like saying, "blah blah, blah blah blah, blah blah?" Well done, son.

Living in hope really comes down to, as a wise Jesuit once told me, whether we approach our world as a place of abundance or scarcity. One way leads to a life of possibilities. The other leaves us recoiled in fetal positions, overcome by a steady onslaught of tepid reader board slogans.

The story of the Feeding of the 5,000 is one of the few miracles that appears in all four Gospels, so clearly it was important to the Gospel writers and early Christian communities. Imagine the scene: A huge crowd has gathered to hear Jesus speak and after a while people start worrying about food, because there isn't any. Some are afraid that a riot might break out. Others suggest that the crowd be ordered to leave before it does.

Jesus responds by asking about the assets on hand. There are only five loaves and two fish. But Jesus doesn't see the "only." Instead of scarcity, Jesus looks upon the assets and sees abundance. The 5,000 are fed, with enough left over for doggie bags.

Or look to a secular story that draws the same distinction. On Christmas Eve a couple placed very different gifts into the stockings of their twins: a precious gold watch in one stocking, horse manure in the other. On Christmas morning, one twin slowly, nervously carried the gold watch into his parents' bedroom. "Mom and Dad, this watch is so beautiful – I'm afraid of breaking it. Is there a safe place to hide it?" Just then the other twin bounded into the bedroom and could barely contain himself as he blurted out, "You won't believe it. Santa brought me a pony. Now I just need to find it!"

Living in abundance is that hopeful way to live that can lead to a truly exceptional life. The fearful who see only scarcity – the hide the watch and crowd can't be fed crowd – often hold sway as the reasonable and prudent. But what kind of life would that be to live? Those folks play small; God didn't make us to play that way.

ON PARENTAL GUILT

I AM OF A GENERATION of dads haunted by the guilt of "Cats in the Cradle."

When you comin' home, dad?
I don't know when – but we'll get together then, son.

But, of course, dad never really does come home. He was always too preoccupied to make time and space for the son while he was growing up. When dad finally does make it home – when he wants to give his kid that time and space – the boy has grown into a man. Now it's dad who is the afterthought. *My boy was just like me.*

I actually don't believe, though, that spending too little time with kids has been a problem for my generation of dads. We always went home – and to every soccer game, recital, and birthday party. Heck, I kept going to grade school Christmas pageants even when the director decided the nativity story wasn't story enough and brought in abstract sets, liturgical dance and new age songs that sounded like everything except Christmas. I was the dad who was always there.

Except when I really wasn't, and that's the soft spot that "Cradle" guilt hits. My thoughts drifted outside home, often occupying work spaces. And so that kid time never felt like enough time, even when I was at home. It was worse when work took me out of town. I carefully avoided oldies radio so that I wouldn't be hit by a Cradle moment. No need to go verklempt while driving to a meeting.

I guarantee that my dad never choked up behind the wheel when Cradle came on. For one, I don't think that he could differentiate songs on the radio. Everything was muzak to him. But mostly it was that life had taught him to not think too much about Cradle stuff. He grew up in northern New Hampshire during the Depression, as a child watched helplessly while his little brother choked to death on a nickel he had swallowed, survived logging camps in Canada as a teenager, fought in Korea, worked his way through college, and then built a life for his family out of nothing. The lyrics to "Cats in the Cradle" were not written in his language.

But they were written in mine. The question for me has been how to not live them.

I once read about a father who made sure that he stopped at his "worry tree" every evening when he came home. He would place his hands on that tree and ask God to implant all the worries of the day into it so that he could really be with his family when he walked through the front door. I liked that story, so I tried the hands-on-tree approach. But not for long.

I just kept forgetting to do it. Probably because I had too many worries on my mind, which is a little ironic. But mostly I stopped because I decided that this ritual might work for others, but not for me. It was because of my dad. I just couldn't picture him embracing a tree outside our home at the end of a work day. This was a guy who, after all, would respond to a no smoking request from travelers who had stopped at his favorite Berlin, New Hampshire, bar with, "You want no smoking? Go to ******* Vermont." My dad didn't hug trees. He cut them down.

But the old man did ultimately help me get a handle on my dad guilt. It happened during the last day of my last visit with him a few years ago. He was confined to bed, and I was sitting next to him for a little while before driving to the airport. We both knew we wouldn't see each other again. My dad wasn't talkative so we watched TV that morning, and the news was filled with the death of Michael Jackson. I was struck by the contrast in the lives of these two men, and proud of the quietly noble and less newsworthy one led by the man lying so still on that bed.

It got me thinking about what it means to be a good man, a good father. Before I walked out the door I asked my dad if he had any advice for me. It took a long time, but finally he wheezed out, "Just keep doing what you're doing I guess."

I didn't need to hear any more than that. There are still a lot of reasons why I don't want our kids to grow up to be "just like me," but not caring enough for them isn't one of them. Time to put the Cradle to bed.

ON FORMATION

I'VE ALWAYS WANTED to be an Andy Taylor kind of dad. Calm and measured. Maintaining perfect equilibrium in all situations. Doling out fatherly advice that's the verbal equivalent of a Norman Rockwell painting.

Sadly, I'm probably cut more from Barney Fife's jib. But, one can dream. And, as I dream about what it would be like to be an Andy Taylor kind of dad, what I think about is formation, that approach to raising children that's all about shaping within.

My favorite *Andy Griffith Show* episode is about a moment in Opie's formation. It's the one when Opie killed a mother bird with his slingshot, leaving her chicks chirping for food in the nest outside his bedroom window. Andy didn't let Opie argue his way out of it, brush it off as "just something that kids do," or wash away Opie's guilt with banal, milque-toasty words. Nope, little Ope had to confront the guilt that came from his reckless act and adhere to consequences.

Opie was required to take responsibility for his action by taking responsibility for the orphaned chicks until they were ready to fly from the nest, the bittersweet conclusion to the episode. Andy's commitment to Opie's formation left open the possibility that Opie's self-esteem would take a hit. Good for Andy. The formation took, and Opie, in those weeks of taking care of the chicks while his father cared for him, discovered something about and within himself. The Opie at the end was shaped differently from the Opie at the beginning.

Which brings me to Willie Wonka, as in, why did anyone ever think that this classic could be improved upon by the Charlie and the Chocolate Factory re-make? And, in that re-make, what made Johnny Depp think he could better Gene Wilder as Willie Wonka, especially with that totally creepy voice that he used? No, a sequel to the original would have held much greater promise, especially if it tracked the lives of all the children not named Charlie after they had left the chocolate factory.

In Willie Wonka, each of the four other children (my favorite is Augustus Gloop) experienced consequences that tied directly to their bad acts – all of them were kicked out of the chocolate factory. But what happened to them after that? Did any of the lessons actually take hold? Maybe those kids took something home that their indulgent parents had never given to them, and maybe that something attached within and a better person came out.

What Willie Wonka started could only be finished by a parent. And without Andy Taylor – and his willingness to do the right thing if not the feel good one – Opie doesn't progress much beyond a somewhat remorseful bird killer. Formation takes two: the child who needs it and the parent who cares enough to walk with that child.

The most famous word in the lexicon of Jesuit discipline is JUG. It is the centuries old term for detention in Jesuit schools and is generally believed to mean "Justice under God." Not so.

The root is actually *"jugum,"* which is Latin for "yoke." And how do most yokes work? There's room for two. A young person who does something wrong takes on the burden of consequences for actions, but the journey isn't taken alone. When a wise adult cares enough to take up the burden with the young person – starting with the moral courage to insist that consequences are better than excuses – real formation happens. A Jesuit I know was fond of saying that "JUG is good for you" to the students he cared for so deeply. He was right.

But formation doesn't just happen with kids. Yes, it takes two, but I've come to learn that there are times when the child is the best teacher and the parent is in need of schooling.

Mrs. Hickey and I, like most parents we know, created a roadmap for our children that included college. This was a given and our minds were locked into this reality. When our middle son began wondering aloud that he might prefer the Army instead, we dismissed it as immature thinking.

He tried college and mostly drifted through his first year without much interest and the feeling that it didn't fit. He brought up the Army to us again, and it was dismissed. He tried again with the same result. That pattern held for a long time.

Then, finally, he sat down with us and presented his full case, and he presented a good one. He explained that the road he needed to travel for himself was not the road we had laid out for him. Then he added that he would only travel down that road if he had our blessing. We began to realize in our heads that he was right, and then that realization took hold in our hearts as well. We gave our blessing.

The child taught the parents. We were in need of formation and our son gave it to us. He did join the Army, and though he agrees that college needs to be part of his journey at some point, he'll choose that path when that's the right turn for him. We had our doubts, of course, but even those melted away when he completed his training as a Combat Medic and we learned its motto, "So Others May Live."

A grace that made St. Ignatius saintly was that he never stopped seeing himself in need of formation. He looked with gratitude at the times in his life when "God taught me as a teacher would teach a student." Like a fish that stops swimming, if we ever see ourselves as fully formed, we die, at least on the inside.

As we grow older we continue to find ways to kill mother birds with slingshots and engorge ourselves in chocolate rivers, and it's a real grace to find ourselves pulling a yoke with God at our side as we step and misstep. God forms now, regardless of our age, just as surely as God formed the first human out of clay. And sometimes God shapes with unexpected hands. My son taught me that.

ON FRIENDSHIP

THE ROMAN AUTHOR TERENCE wrote that, "I am human and consider nothing human alien to me." Add to Terence that, because we humans are made in God's image, the more human we are the closer we are to God. Then pile on a little more: nothing makes us more human than deep, lasting friendships. It holds, therefore, that friendships are imbued with the sacred, a taste of God. (Quite the syllogism – my logic teacher would have been so proud.)

My favorite saints are the most human ones, especially those who valued friendships. Look at St. Ignatius. He founded the Society of Jesus with his college buddies from the University of Paris, and their lives together reflected those early bonds. So, for example, when Ignatius was leading the Jesuits in Rome, it was often the case that "raucous laughter" could be heard from behind closed doors during meetings. The early Jesuits valued relationships so much that they even wrote a rule – one still followed today – that a social can never be skipped. On the more personal side, one of the great treasures from those early days remains with us today: tear-stained letters between Ignatius and Francis Xavier, best friends separated by the many miles between Rome and India.

Or look to another favorite of mine, St. Teresa of Avila. One day her saddle slipped as she was crossing a stream and she found herself stuck under the belly of her donkey. She complained to God and heard, "Teresa, whom the Lord loves He chastises. This is how I treat my friends." To which Teresa replied, "Which is why you have so few."

I like saints who trash talk a bit, even with God. And the best friendships often sound the same way.

When we were in our late 20s and 30s, a group of friends from high school and college gathered every summer for The He-Man, a grueling three day athletic competition. To the winners went the He-Man trophy. The losers wore plastic turds around their necks.

Last summer we resurrected the He-Man after a 20 year hiatus. A couple events did match the intensity of early He-Man competitions (basketball and a 5K muddy obstacle course some of us ran). But the resurrected version also reflected middle age with events like Jeopardy (including the categories of Marquette basketball and *The Rockford Files*) and par three golf (with carts). Even so, one of us still managed to tear his achilles, which resulted in his being ignominiously carted around Milwaukee throughout the He-Man, plastic turd on full display.

What's best about these times together is that we always pick up right where we left off. The stories are the same (as our wives remind us) and pretty much the jokes are too. One of the great pleasures and treasures in life is to have friends so close that every reference is immediately understood and nothing ever needs to be explained. I mention to a buddy, for example, how badly I still feel about "accidentally" spilling that beer on his head during a boat ride and, without fail for 30 years, the response is always, "Remind me to break your arm like a chicken wing." And no hugs are required or desired when greeting after years of separation. "Hey, nice shirt. When did you start sewing your own clothes?" will do fine.

A few months after "He-Man Resurrection," one of our He-Man buddies unexpectedly died from a massive stroke. Friends gathered in Wisconsin once again, and there were tears of separation at the wake and then raucous laughter when the post-wake turned into the Irish kind. There was also an unspoken understanding that memories were no longer enough. We needed to make new ones and attach a greater commitment to our great friendships.

"We are not human beings having a spiritual experience. We are spiritual beings having a human experience," wrote Teilhard de Chardin S.J. There's the link between the human and divine again. I'm so glad for that. We don't end when our bodies do; the spiritual, which is who we are, continues on. *Vita mutatur, non tollitur.* Life is changed, not ended.

I was thinking about that Latin phrase during my friend's funeral. I smiled when it struck me that it would have really irked my friend that I was thinking about a Latin phrase during his funeral. I don't know Latin. I just used to throw out Latin phrases at him when we were roommates in law school so that he would threaten to break my arm like a chicken wing.

Then I smiled a little wider, knowing that it would irk him a little more, when another Latin phrase hit me: *Amicitia mutatur, non tollitur.* Friendship is changed, not ended.

The Irish tell of a thin space where the divine resides and we occasionally step into. I will look for my friend there.

ON DOGMATISM

LES MISERABLES is my favorite musical. It has both wonderful songs and a great story line, all centered around the struggle between Javert and Jean Valjean.

Javert is a police inspector whose fanatical devotion to the letter of the law is challenged by the humanity of Jean Valjean. Encounters with that humanity appear to draw Javert into empathy and chip away at his absolutist approach to life. Ultimately, however, his dogmatism is irresolvable and, faced with the possibility of living without it, Javert chooses to not live at all.

Dogmatism is riding on the top rail right now. Understandably so in uncertain times. There's great comfort in simple solutions to every problem. Life is just easier when lived by a fool-proof playbook, one that comes with labels to stick on apostates who deviate from The Truth.

Mastery of that playbook means you know all the answers, a righteousness readily embraced by the disciples of dogmatism. Every age has them. Jesus railed against the temple priests and scribes, the dogmatists of his time. Rabbi Hillel, who lived shortly before Jesus, had a succinct response for those who wished to substitute law for faith: "What is hateful to you, do not do to your neighbor. That is the whole Torah, the rest is commentary."

Both spoke to the great sin of dogmatism: elevating doctrine above people. It's the sin of selfishness really, the arrogance of egoism. Dogmatic personalities are more annoying than damaging in most circumstances. However, on violent extremes dogmatism can provide ideological justification for the pure to subjugate the impure, regardless of the label type. There was no real difference between, for example, Hitler (fascist, right) and Stalin (communist, left).

Is there a cure for dogmatism? There's likely none for the truly rabid. But for others a start would be visiting bigger, messier places where people of varied views can actually get to know each other. This knowledge might even lead to empathy, a willingness to walk that mile in another's shoes.

Trying on those shoes and walking around is a big part of what college is about, or at least should be about. Instead, college campuses often reflect the trend to look only for one's own image and listen to only one's own voice. But, of course, that has nothing to do with real learning, which has as its ultimate goals the attainment of wisdom and empathy, becoming a more human human.

As interesting as Javert's dilemma is to ponder, I think there is an even better literary character to consider as a counter-point to dogmatism: Huck Finn, a mostly illiterate boy. You don't get much more dogmatic than the antebellum South, what with the rigid stance of slavery as a divinely ordered institution and the belief that black people were less human than white people. Huck is of this order and lives it, until he starts to journey with Jim and eventually encounters that transcendent moment when the friend who needs his help trumps the doctrine of his time.

Ultimately, a dogmatic approach to life binds one up in its own kind of slavery. But freedom can be grasped when we see and embrace the human at our side.

Judging others makes us blind, whereas love is illuminating. By judging others we blind ourselves to our own evil and to the grace which others are just as entitled to as we are.
-Dietrich Bonhoeffer, from *The Cost of Discipleship*

ON GOODNESS

A GENEROUS, CONSCIENTIOUS TEENAGER was trying very hard to live a life full of goodness. He followed all the rules, didn't cheat or lie, was respectful to his parents and was kind to others. Even so, he sensed that more was needed for that goodness to really take hold and flourish. So he sought out a wise man for advice.

What we also know about this young man, in the story from Luke's gospel, was that he was rich. So the account is always referred to as the Story of The Rich Young Man, which I think is a distraction because the story isn't really about being rich.

It is true that Jesus saw riches as being a problem for this young man, something that was keeping him from fully embracing the goodness that resided within. And it's also true that Jesus told the young man he needed to give those possessions away to the poor and then follow him. As recounted in Luke, the young man's "face fell" as he turned and went away. Jesus was asking much of him.

But it's also recounted in Luke's gospel that when Jesus first saw the young man he looked into his face and loved him. Just as Jesus immediately sensed that possessions were a problem, he also sensed that this was just a great kid standing in front of him. He gave that kid a hard choice to make, asking much of him because Jesus knew there was much to him. And it's that choice that this story is really about.

A few years ago I was at a Mass celebrated by a Cardinal, and he spoke about this story. He described how sad the lad must have been as he left Jesus, "forever exiled from His presence." The Cardinal suggested that with that one decision the boy had cast his lot with "riches, power, and sex." How he was able to weave sex into the story I do not know, but I do know one thing about what the Cardinal said: He was dead wrong.

No one outside the grave is "forever exiled" from the presence of God. No one decision forever condemns anyone to a life of evil, nor does one decision guarantee a lifetime of goodness. Every day brings both the opportunity and responsibility to choose whether or not to embrace goodness, and most of those choices are small ones. They don't make their way into the news or into a gospel, but that doesn't mean they aren't important. Each day we make ourselves more of what we are becoming by the choices we make.

The most natural choice for us to make is to choose goodness, because we are by nature good. Look to that first creation story in Genesis. Each day, day after day, God creates; and each day, day after day, God looks at what was created and says it is good. But on the last day of creation, something changes. God creates humans, looks at us and pronounces that we are "very good."

So, that "very goodness" is already within us and, the more we choose good, the more good we make and the better we become. Goodness grows within and also without. *"Bonum est diffusuvum sui."* Goodness tends to spread, said St. Thomas Aquinas. Think of goodness kind of like The Force from Star Wars. Goodness is a living thing, so it grows when fed and withers when starved. This is so within ourselves and also so for any community or nation.

And, although Aquinas didn't say this and I suspect my Latin is really bad, evil works the same way: *"Malum est diffusuvum sui."* Malice, evil, also tends to spread. Using Tolkien and *The Lord of the Rings* for the popular culture reference this time around, evil is the shadow that dark acts cause to lengthen and, in turn, is darkness itself that overcomes light as it lengthens. Acts and is acted upon. Even inaction grows the shadow. Edmund Burke said that, "The only thing necessary for the triumph of evil is for good men to do nothing." Doing nothing is a choice that can be just as damaging as the decision to put a ring on a finger or not.

Could it really be that straightforward? Yes. Every day in simple ways.

A terrific diocesan priest I know tells the story of a senior who stood up at the final retreat of the year and told his classmates how happy he was to be with them, because he nearly wasn't. Freshman year was incredibly hard on him, at home and at school. He felt so overwhelmed that on one Friday at the end of the school day he packed up the contents of his locker, stuffed them in his bag, and walked out the front door of the school, determined to never return.

On the way out he dropped his bag and everything spilled out to the ground. Most walked by, inactive. A couple laughed. But one girl, an upperclassman, didn't. She bent down and helped him pick up his stuff. Then she went outside with him and they walked together to his bus stop, talking along the way. As she left him, she turned and asked, "See you on Monday, right?" No answer. She wouldn't take no-answer as his answer, so she asked again, "See you on Monday?" "Yes," the freshman said, and he did.

That freshman ended up having a wonderful high school experience. But he told his classmates during that senior retreat that he almost didn't. On that fateful Friday he had planned to run away from his home and from school, never to return. That's how horrible he felt, how fully he loathed himself, and how much pain he was in. He just wanted to be somewhere else, be anybody else. It was hard for his classmates to believe, since they had really only known him as a friendly, thoughtful, and good person who enjoyed life.

But, he said, that senior girl "saved me that day." And how did she do it? She helped him pick up some books, talked and walked with him a bit, made sure that he was worth seeing again that coming Monday. Little ways to do good that carried with them a wondrous way to spread goodness.

Let's finish where we began – that rich young man. Jesus loved him and challenged him: what you own is owning you. The young man's face fell and he went away sad. But he wasn't forever exiled from God's presence or forever prohibited from choosing goodness. That was just that day; what happened the next day?

Just maybe that next day the young man showed up and had breakfast with Jesus, less encumbered with the possessions that had been weighing him down and full of the certain belief that Jesus had seen great goodness within him, a goodness that could now be freely shared in a lifetime of doing good.

THINKING OF YOU KENT

ON MY TROPHY LIFE

I LIKE TO KEEP remembrances of places we've lived on my desk at home. One of my favorites is a photo of a friend's dog leaving a parting gift on the front lawn of our Seattle home shortly after we had moved to a new neighborhood.

Another favorite is a trophy that was given to me by my old basketball buddies in Milwaukee when we moved to Seattle in 1999. It's a Sportsmanship Award, in recognition of the outstanding character I displayed throughout my playing years. I'm pretty sure it was one of those not-so-hidden message type gifts.

I've struggled with an overly-competitive zeal all my life. Some would call it enthusiasm, most correctly recognize it as annoying or pathetic. Yes, I was "that guy" on the soccer pitch and the basketball court. Even to this day one of those Milwaukee buddies reminds me of how I had shouldered him so hard during a game that he flew into the adjacent court. Did I mention that he's a Jesuit priest?

I'd like to say that becoming a parent transformed me from "that guy" to a better guy, but there are a lot of things I'd like to say that just aren't true. There was, for example, that nerf soccer game for five year olds in a small gym that comes to mind. Our son – to my great annoyance – was more focused on talking with other players than playing the game. "Just let it go. Kids' game," I repeated to myself in my head. And then I heard some jerk yell out, just as the parents had gone quiet, "STOP MESSING AROUND AND GO TO THE BALL!"

The look from Mrs. Hickey suggested that the jerk was me. I tried to draw condemning eyes to the guy next to me by turning a disapproving stare toward him. No takers. My walk of shame back to the car after the game was a solitary one.

That event taught me a lesson, as did years of being an administrator and coach at high schools. Parent complaints – and I've heard a lot of them – are almost always about their kids' playing time (even if they are disguised as something else). But they are borne in that overly-competitive place that I know well.

We mock the "Participation" trophies on our kids' shelves. Young people today are even referred to as the "Trophy Generation." But, if that is true, why should they be blamed? Those trophies came from somewhere, did they not? Most likely those shelves are filled by parents who are trying to fill up something missing from their own mantles, or perhaps their own lives.

A man should go where he won't be tempted. So, I've tried to stay away from trophy hunting over the years. I still have those moments when my competitiveness kicks into overdrive and I feel like hurling something through the air, like maybe a Jesuit. Thankfully, though, those moments are now few and far between. I just don't want to be "that guy" anymore and, thankfully, I've mellowed. Life itself blesses us with perspective.

And life also blesses us with companions who help us gain that perspective. I am thankful for words I heard 20 years ago from a good Jesuit friend, words I still keep tacked to a bulletin board at work. Increasingly frustrated by my overly competitive zeal and how I was treating others, I asked for a cure. He answered with a question: "For what are you willing to crucify someone?"

I haven't found that "what" – then or now – and pray that I never do.

ON GOD

TIM TEBOW was a flash in the pan quarterback sensation for the Denver Broncos a few years ago. Tremendously athletic, he found ways to win on a wing and a prayer, pulling victories out of his backside. Also tremendously Christian, Tebow attributed every win to God, all part of an intelligent design. His sideline prayer stance – "Tebowing" – even became a thing that youngsters throughout the country emulated.

Saturday Night Live spoofed Tebow-Mania with a skit that also raised the theological question of where God is to be found in human events. Tebow, in the locker room after another dramatic win, thanks God for making it all happen. Then Jesus appears: "Here's the thing. If we're going to keep doing this, you gotta meet me halfway out there.... It's not a good week if every week, I, the Son of God, have to come in, drop everything, and bail out the Denver Broncos in the fourth quarter. I'm a busy guy. So, before every game, stretch. Get the arm warm. Read the playbook."

I think about that skit and that question about where God fits whenever my beloved Packers visit Seattle to take on the Seahawks. The Packers find strange ways to lose, to which Russell Wilson points a finger to God. Aaron Rodgers, the Packers quarterback, sees it differently: God is probably not so interested in scheming the outcomes of football games.

Does God determine outcomes or does God leave that mostly to us? There's support for both positions in the Bible, especially in the Pentateuch, the first five books in Hebrew Scriptures.

God is the primary author of the Bible, but God certainly had the help of inspired human authors. Scholars have identified four primary authors (or sources) of the Pentateuch, two of them are the Priestly and Yahwist writers. Separated by centuries, their writings were once independent sources. Many centuries ago, biblical editors wove their accounts into the books we have today. But we can still hear their distinct voices within those books, and one way to tell them apart is their very different perceptions of God.

The Priestly writer, author of the first creation story, describes God as totally in control as creation is created in those six days. Later, in Exodus, God "hardens" the heart of Pharaoh, thus forcing the conclusion that God desires – the destruction of the Egyptian army and freedom for the Israelites. God directs outcomes, and humans play out a divine script.

The Yahwist had a very different take on God. In the second creation story, God gets into the dirt and breathes life into the human. Adam and Eve then go on to choose the evil that results in their expulsion from the Garden. In Exodus, the decisions made by Pharaoh and Moses are made by them, not forced upon them. God cares, but doesn't control.

Maybe those contrasting perspectives were woven together by biblical editors to prompt us to consider something closer to the middle: God walks with us in life, but where we go is pretty much up to us. The Yahwist captured that image of God in Genesis 3, when God strolls about the Garden of Eden looking for Adam and Eve during the "breezy time of day." Of course, the reason why God has to look for them is that they are hiding behind their newly realized nakedness. They are expelled from the garden – no more strolls with God – and that expulsion is of their own making due to their own choices. A traumatic event for them, but what about the trauma that God experienced?

A lot of crazy, often violent things have happened in this world because of someone or some nation claiming to know the mind of God. However, it's also true that a lot of crazy, violent stuff happens when we don't know God. To me, trying to know God is both a head and heart thing, something to study and something to feel. I had an experience of both in a course I took in college.

It was called "Atheism and Theism," and the first part of the course was an immersion in atheistic thought. A life-long Catholic, I was surprised when I found myself seeing the logic of that position. Those arguments denying God's existence were highly persuasive and they took hold in my head more and more as the semester moved along. I slowly came to the intellectual realization that God didn't exist, and this made me feel anxious and even anguished as I began to sense what this meant.

This all came to a climax on a cold, gray Milwaukee morning as I walked to class. My body was bent against the wind and under the weight of the God existence question. At one point I stopped at a street corner piled up with black exhaust snow, and I just stood there. Then I decided deep with conviction what I had been thinking in my head, maybe even saying it out loud: "That's it. There is no God."

What happened right after that is hard to describe, but it is the clearest memory I possess. "But don't you know how much I love you." That's what I heard inside me. I know I didn't hear that with my ears, but also know it wasn't something I had thought to myself. The words were both internal and distinct from me, if that makes sense.

The best words I've found to describe the feeling I had are from a line in a prayer of Ignatius Loyola, the *Anima Christi* ("Soul of Christ"): "Blood of Christ, inebriate me." I was inebriated by the certain sense of God's love for me. I stood on that corner and just cried, I don't know for how long. I've never felt so much joy before or since.

I could not say that every decision I've made, every word I've said, and every thing I've done has flowed from that memory. To my frustration, disappointment, and shame, so much of my life has actually run contrary to that experience. But, what has remained with me is the certainty that God wants to be with me, to take strolls in the garden together. It's up to me to decide whether to go there or not, and I think that God is hurt when I decide to stay away. Yes, I believe that God has feelings, including feelings for me.

The theologian, Henri Nouwen, once said that, "The unfathomable mystery of God is that God is a Lover who wants to be loved." That love is personal, not theoretical, and the Lover that is God is always present. How God works in this world remains a mystery. What is not a mystery is that God does.

ON MAKING MISTAKES

ONE OF THE BEST scenes in *The Shawshank Redemption* involves Red, an old man who has lived most of his life in prison, telling a parole board what he would say to his younger self:

"I look back on the way I was then: a young stupid kid who committed a terrible crime. I want to try to talk some sense to him, tell him the way things are."

I think of what Red said when a young kid gets into trouble for doing something stupid, something that happens every school year. There are many reasons for stupid behavior. I recall a student, for example, who was brought up for expulsion because a knife fell out of her purse during class. I didn't expel her. Turns out that that she planned to go to the mall after school and her father had given a knife to her just in case she needed it. That was stupid, meaning that it was really stupid of that daughter to have listened to such a really stupid father.

The biggest problem with teenagers is their brains, which are also one of the best things about teenagers. The teenage brain has so much more than the adult brain, but also less, especially less judgment. Now add in for good measure extreme teenage insecurity and angst. That's a dangerous elixir swirling around in that head: "Do you like me? Would you if I were outrageous?" It's all a recipe for mistake-making, and with cellphones today it's all captured for posterity and for all the world to see.

One way we could help teenagers is to try to find ways to reduce the chances of those mistakes happening in the first place. Heads holding teenage brains may lack judgment, but that doesn't mean they're empty. One thing they are full of is socialization.

A few years ago in Spain someone observed a sheep jumping off a cliff and, sure enough, all the other sheep followed. While that's not exactly the kind of socialization that's needed, the fact is that teenagers are pretty good at reinforcing with each other consistent social messages that make sense to them as basic guidelines. Something in between "Blindly follow the herd" and "Apply that reservoir of life experiences and analytical skills to work out that problem on your own."

Many of us of a certain age, for example, came to believe that only we could prevent forest fires because Smokey the Bear had told us so, and we stopped littering because we saw that Chief crying on the side of a highway. Teenagers these days don't drink and drive as much as their parents did, wear seatbelts more regularly, and have seen enough bad teeth pictures to avoid meth. Just because they think differently doesn't mean they don't think. Teenagers can and do learn how to navigate growing up, including use of social media, as long as they get a little help along the way.

Will clear, consistent and constantly communicated social mores eliminate teenage mistakes? Oh, Lord, absolutely not. And that's a really good thing. It turns out that making mistakes and failing can carry – in the right circumstances – the enormous benefit of character building. It also turns out that character, much more than IQ and test scores, is the best indicator of success in life.

It's a wonder that anyone survives adolescence. Not one of us looks back at our high school years and doesn't grimace. Stupid things said and so many awkward moments of self-doubt and struggling to fit in, compounded by bad judgment. As I'm fond of saying to parents – though they may not be so fond of hearing from me – no one goes through high school unscarred. Believe it or not, that's a good thing.

ON STAYING HUMAN

AN ANONYMOUS HOLOCAUST survivor had seen horrible atrocities committed by educated people – college graduates, nurses, engineers and doctors – in a concentration camp. He wrote:

> *I'm suspicious of education.*
> *My request is: help your students to be human.*
> *Your efforts must never produce learned monsters,*
> *skilled psychopaths, or educated Eichmanns.*
> *Reading, writing, spelling, history and arithmetic are only*
> *important*
> *if they serve to make our students human.*

Being human is not a gift to be taken for granted, but, of course, we do. One reason is that we just don't have to work very hard to become human. I, for one, have no recollection of having put forth much effort during either my conception or my birth.

And I also don't recall having done much to be called very good. Yet, there you have it, right in Genesis. God creates humans and immediately tags us with the "very good" label. High praise indeed given how little effort we put into it.

The trick is staying that way. Staying human seems to take a lot of effort.

I recall a day during my junior year in college when it hit me that I wasn't being a very good human; I was treating others poorly and felt badly about this. So, I resolved to go to Confession, and that's what I did.

I went to Gesu Church in Milwaukee and watched carefully as the Jesuits came out of the sacristy and walked toward their confession booths. I was very embarrassed about what I had to say, so I looked for the perfect priest: mostly deaf, preferably senile.

Jackpot. I spotted my man: Hearing aid and very old – I pegged him at 137. As he shuffled inside his booth, I bee-lined to his line. I may or may not have bumped a nun out of the way to get to the front of the line. Didn't matter to me. I was going to Confession; I just added it to the list.

I knelt in that dark booth and in that darkness I confessed my sins to a face I couldn't see. (This took a while.) Then I stopped. Dead Silence. Had the priest rewarded himself with a nap? Had he gone on to his eternal reward?

Finally, that ancient Jesuit spoke the words that would change my life: "Well," he said, "you're just a BIG IDIOT." I didn't see that coming. Then he proceeded to tell me why I was a BIG IDIOT. And he was right.

I have a lot of reasons to be thankful for that experience. For one, I'm thankful I didn't ignore that bad feeling I felt when I was treating others badly. The conscience helps us to stay human, but only if we listen.

I'm also really thankful for that old priest. How many confessions had he heard in his life from BIG IDIOT college students? Yet, he still took the time to care. We have enough people in our lives who take the easy way and tell us what we want to hear. Better to find some people who care enough to tell us what we need to hear.

Finally, I'm thankful that I had the sense to kneel down. That's what you do in a confessional, but I don't do it enough. A holy man once said, "There are thousands of ways to kneel and kiss the ground." Kneeling to ask for forgiveness is just one way; each day there are so many more. Every space can be sacred, and every face may contemplate the divine. We turn a street corner and suddenly there's a burning bush, but we're usually too busy to see it, let alone take to knees.

I think about Nazis every once in a while. How does someone become a Nazi? I don't mean membership cards or loyalty oaths, but how it is that a "very good" human can become something so bad. Those monsters who committed such atrocities during the Holocaust had birthdays, went to schools, and had wonderful graduation ceremonies where everyone told them what remarkable humans they were. So why didn't they stay that way?

I think it's because they forgot how to kneel, or maybe just didn't see the need. They became too self-absorbed for awe; refused to see God's face in another's face; walked on by one burning bush after another. Then there finally came a day when they looked into a mirror and saw a god looking back. And from then on it was only before a mirror that they would kneel.

And that's how monsters are made.

ON THE FRANCIS EFFECT

THE BEST THING about our Jesuit pope is how Jesuit he is. From the earliest days, the Jesuits talked about "our way of proceeding," a way grounded in the Spiritual Exercises of St. Ignatius. It's a culture (or what Jesuits call "charism") that defies simple categorizations like left or right. Pope Francis fully reflects that charism in his leadership. It's impossible to deconstruct his message into categories, though the pundits never seem to tire from trying.

Is Francis a closet Marxist? Theologically traditional or progressive? Socially conservative or liberal? It's impossible to pin this guy down.

The pundits were similarly lost 2,000 years ago. Who was this Jesus? The Zealots wanted him to be more political, the establishment in the Sanhedrin less so. Some of the Pharisees (early adopters of clericalism) thought Jesus should be harder on the people with rules. Many would-be disciples found even his few simple rules too hard to live by.

Jesus would remain an enigma until a few followers started to piece together that everything he did and talked about flowed from the Shema, the core of Mosaic Law: Love God with all your heart, soul and might (Dt. 6:4). To which Jesus added, as the second greatest commandment, "…and your neighbor as yourself."

Jesus' response when asked about paying taxes would have been right out of the Francis playbook (if Jesus hadn't already written it): Give to Caesar what is Caesar's and to God what is God's. What belongs to God is our hearts. We give that place away too cheaply when we replace what resides there – God's deepest desires for us – with soul-killing substitutes.

I think that's the key to Francis: The placement of God first and foremost, which places the person, who is made in God's image, also first and foremost. It is the religious humanism at the core of Jesuit spirituality. Take that as the starting point, and Francis' endpoints make sense.

That means that there is no place for any economic ideology on the left or right that places materialism at the heart instead of God.

No Socialism and no trickle-down Capitalism. Maybe Francis would go with a Capitalism-With-Questions: "How is the worker in the work treated? Where is the promotion of the common good? What will you do with what you have?"

There is a difference, for example, between the ethos of a Costco compared to Walmart, and it isn't just the $1.50 Polish Sausage. There is also a difference between what the Gates family is doing with its wealth (eradicating disease) and what that punky hedge fund manager who bought himself a pharmaceutical company a few years ago and then raised the price of a life-saving pill from $13.50 to $750 (increasing disease) did with his money.

If God and the human faces made in God's image serve as the foundation for Francis, then the lessons he teaches, though politically disjointed, are actually seamlessly consistent. How can the life of the unborn child be connected with the impoverishment wrought by global warming? Given Francis' starting point, how can they not be?

"Marxist ideology is wrong, but I have met many Marxists in my life who are good people." Classic Bergoglio (Francis). So too is the story of one of the great women in the life of Francis, Esther Ballestrino de Careaga, the atheist/communist who supervised a young Bergoglio in a science lab for three years.

In 1977, Esther and some French nuns were abducted by the Argentine military from a Church where they were holding a human rights meeting. Esther's remains were found in 2005 and Esther's

daughter asked Cardinal Bergoglio if she could be buried in the garden of that Church. He, of course, said yes.

And that is how the body of an atheist/communist ended up in the sacred ground of a Buenos Aires Catholic Church. A seemingly strange ending place, but not if we understand its beginning: "I owed a lot to that woman. I loved her a lot."

"NO, I'M NOT TALKING ABOUT TWITTER.
I LITERALLY WANT YOU TO FOLLOW ME."

ON RAPTUROUS LIVING

I HAVE A BIG PROBLEM with "The Rapture," but believe in rapturing.

By "The Rapture," I mean the belief that pops up every once in a while that the world is about to end and a chosen few will be taken up. While not mentioned in the Bible, it is derived from apocalyptic literature such as the Book of Revelation. I have no problem with rapture talk when spoken by honest believers. What irks me is when it's used by scam artists to make a lot of money, thus separating the gullible from theirs and reducing Christianity to late night talk show jokes.

The manipulative cruelty of this cosmic con game hurts real people. I remember, for example, the picture of a poor sap who bought what the hucksters had been selling about an upcoming rapture date and time, had sold off his retirement savings to get the word out, and then stood by helplessly as a Times Square crowd mocked him when he was still hanging around as the proclaimed rapture time passed.

I do believe there will be an end time. I just don't think that much good comes from constantly speculating about it or joining survivalist colonies. Jesus gave the best answer when he was asked about when the end would come: No one knows, so be prepared for it at any time. Preparation doesn't entail selling off 401(k) plans or building bomb shelters. Jesus is clear that the best way to prepare for the end time is by answering a fundamental question in the present time: Will you follow me?

And that's why I believe in rapturing, or at least my definition of rapturing, which I see as answering "yes" to the follow-Jesus question. It's a verb, not a noun. It requires a response, but there is something strange about what that response requires. Saying "yes" to the follow-Jesus question carries with it an immediacy that is shocking to the system, ripping the responder out of one life story and into another.

Here's what I mean by that, as described in Luke 9:59-62: One would-be follower says he'll come along with Jesus after he says goodbye to his family. Jesus calls him unfit because he wants to look to what he left behind. Another potential follower says that he will be there just as soon as he finishes burying his dead father. No time for that, Jesus says. "Let the dead bury the dead." Huh? That kind of response makes no sense in the real world, which is maybe the point Jesus was trying to make.

There's a great line in a Leonard Cohen (RIP) song: "He (Jesus) sank beneath your wisdom like a stone." I think the "wisdom" he referred to was the wisdom of the world. There's something clearly unwise (and even absurd) about following Jesus, especially when we think about really strange notions like the Incarnation and Crucifixion. And yet, there we have it, the choice between the wisdom that is affirmed by the world and the wisdom that doesn't seem wise at all.

If, despite this, we still decide to follow Jesus, we are then asked to take a step further. Following Jesus means becoming a citizen of the Kingdom. But, get how Jesus describes what that means: "…the Kingdom of heaven suffers violence, and the violent bear it away." (Mt. 11:12)

Jesus portrays the Kingdom as strife-ridden and those violent bearers as the good guys. That doesn't jive well with what we normally think of the Kingdom (butterflies and flowery fields) or disciples (who, in the *Godspell* version of the story, are clowns and, even worse, mimes). There's something unseemly, even dangerous about the Kingdom, and this decision to follow Jesus feels threatening. Let the dead bury the dead.

When I teach Scripture, I ask students to make sense of two short parables: First, the Kingdom of Heaven is like leaven hidden in flour that rises; and, second, the Kingdom of Heaven is like a small mustard seed that grows into a large bush. They immediately get the concept that the Kingdom starts out small and gets larger. But it's not that simple or that safe.

Leaven was viewed as corruptive, created out of food that had spoiled and gone bad. The mustard seed grew into a plant that was a massive, invasive weed, something to be guarded against and separated from good plants in the garden. Yet, the Kingdom of Heaven is like these things?

One of the great lines C. S. Lewis uses over and over in the *Narnia Chronicles* concerns the nature of Aslan, the Lion-Jesus figure in those wonderful stories: "Aslan is not a tame lion." I recall that there was a big disagreement between the owners of the film rights to the *Narnia Chronicles*, with one faction holding out that more profit could be realized if the Christian themes were removed. Luckily, that faction lost out. One of the key themes in those stories is that there is nothing tame about Jesus and nothing safe about Christianity. They only become docile when the wisdom of the world (think marketing focus groups) replaces God's wisdom (which sinks beneath it like a stone).

Let's go back to that poor soul waiting for the rapture on Times Square. I felt sorry for that man, but also admired him. He would have been better off if he had listened to what Jesus had to say about the end times instead of the hucksters, but at least he acted upon the strength of his conviction, which is more than can be said for most of us. Or at least for me.

A few years ago I saw another man on a corner looking foolish, this time at a busy intersection on the Strip in Las Vegas. I had stopped at the intersection while walking back to my hotel after a night when the luck of the Irish had not been with me, and I noticed a boisterous crowd had gathered there. A street preacher stood on a box, calling for repentance and following Jesus (rapturing the verb). He was heckled loudly and profanely and, though the preacher responded to the hecklers bravely, he was a pitiable figure as he faced the onslaught alone. It felt really uncomfortable, and even...violent. A guilty bystander, I didn't say or stand on anything. I crossed the street and walked back to my hotel.

The end of the world is going to come some day, but when it will come no one can know. What is known is that we might see the face of God anytime, so that "follow me" question needs to be answered every time it's asked. And it is asked by the strangest people in the most unexpected places.

ON JUDGING

ONE DAY I WAS WALKING with a friend when I was suddenly attacked by a crow. It swooped down at my head over and over, and I finally had to run away and shelter in place.

It was likely just a case of mistaken identity, since the friend I was walking with is named Jay and it's well known that crows don't like jays. So, I didn't worry too much about it. But later I was told that I had now been marked by that crow and should expect more attacks in the future. The battle was on, and I decided to arm myself with all the information about crows I could extract from Wikipedia.

I had never liked crows – pesky and noisy rats-with-wings that they are – and now had even more reason to despise them. What I read about crows, however, changed my opinion of them. It turns out that crows are playful, highly intelligent, and social. They care for each other and fearlessly protect their families. It's likely that I was attacked because I had walked by a nest. So I came to see crows in a more favorable light, while fastidiously avoiding the attack zone for a while.

This experience reminded me of a maxim of St. Ignatius: "Interpret another's actions in a light most favorable to that person." It's so easy for us – or at least for me – to automatically interpret something others have said or done in the worst light first, and then perhaps give them the chance to prove otherwise later on. Ignatius, calling for more generous, open hearts, flipped that approach on its head.

Let's move from crows to mockingbirds. It seems to me that two characters from *To Kill a Mockingbird*, Tom Robinson and Boo Radley, were attacked because of tendencies to interpret the actions of another in the least favorable light. Many of the white townspeople, for example, assumed that Tom Robinson had raped a white girl because that's the kind of thing black men did to white women. And the three children at the center of the story, including Scout, assumed that Boo Radley was a monstrous threat to them because he was crazy and that's what crazy people did.

Toward the end of the novel, the evidence clearly showed that the actions of both Tom Robinson and Boo Radley were actually most kind and even noble. Still, the white townspeople, hearts hardened, refused to see Tom Robinson's actions as anything but sinister. His life was ruined. Conversely, the children, especially Scout, were open-hearted enough to come to see Boo Radley's actions in a most favorable light, that they were borne out of a good, though misunderstood, soul.

At that time the disciples approached Jesus and said, "Who is the greatest in the kingdom of heaven?" He called a child over, placed it in their midst, and said, "Amen, I say to you, unless you turn and become like children, you will not enter the kingdom of heaven."
    -Mt. 18: 1-3

ON FINDING MEANING IN VEGAS

I DON'T KNOW WHY I had it in mind that I would suffer a mid-life crisis when I hit my 50th birthday. I just assumed that I would. Isn't that what people do? My birthday came, and then went. No crisis. I seemed pretty happy, enjoying my life and grateful for the people in it. Was there something wrong with me? Was I not taking this huge life change as seriously as I should?

The fact that I didn't feel a mid-life crisis happening made me feel nervous that I wasn't having one. Better, I thought, to head this off at the pass. Resolve my mid-life crisis before it started. So, I decided to embark on a journey for meaning to find the key to purposeful living. But where exactly does one go to find real answers to a fake crisis?

Vegas seemed to be a perfect destination for my quest. Some good friends, concerned about the emotional toll my phony crisis was taking on me, gave this trip to me as a birthday gift (including first class plane tickets!). The trip was a huge success, as documented in the photo journal below.

So many thoughts raced through my head as we prepared for takeoff. That separation curtain, for example, seemed pretty flimsy. How committed were the flight attendants to keeping Coach passengers out of the First Class restroom? Should I get a refund for my recently concluded tanning sessions? And, most importantly, how would I find out the key to a purposeful life during my trip?

Then it hit me: I would just ask! Vegas must be a mecca for those searching for life's meaning. Why else would anyone go there? It followed, then, that the best people to ask about the purpose of life would be those who lived and worked in Vegas. So, that's what I did.

I had a terrific waiter while dining at Caesar's Palace. Brian had a very ready answer to my question, "What is the key to a purposeful life?" Brian said, "No one controls your moods but you." He explained how each night he would deal with great customers and really bad customers. If he let those bad ones control his work, his mood, and his outlook, then he would be surrendering his life to them.

Joanne took a lot of time before she responded to my question and then thoughtfully stated, "It's better to have an open mind than an open purse." I had no idea what Joanne was talking about. So, I went back to playing blackjack with the credit line I'd arranged with the Jesuit Relief Fund for Administrators Suffering from a Mid-Life Crisis.

Though young in age, Paula, a poolside waitress, was wise indeed. She was emphatic in making the point, one similar to Brian's view, that you just can't let comments made to you or about you weigh you down. "Don't ever take anything personally!" – a point Paula emphasized with direct language and direct finger pointing.

I really enjoyed a terrific poolside performance by The Super Cr3w, a dance group that has won many awards and even performed at the White House. While watching them, the thought hit me, "Maybe this is where I am being called in order to live a purposeful life!" So, I arranged a tryout.

Candidly, it didn't go well. Apparently Super Cr3w requires greater athleticism than I possess, like the ability to do more than kneel on the ground in a dance pose without actually moving. But, the guys

still gave me a cool parting gift: A lesson in the official team hand signal! They also shared with me the equally cool team motto: "Stay Clean. Stay Consistent. Stay Creative." That's the key, they said, when I asked them my purpose of life question: "Keep it real."

In keeping with Ignatian spiritual practices, toward the end of my trip, I paused to reflect upon what I had learned in my quest to find purpose. Vegas style. So, I cozied up in front of the fireplace channel on the TV in my room and reflected on my experience.

Though I had made up my mid-life crisis, there was nothing made up about my conversations with the good people I met who worked in Vegas.

They had fun with the purposeful life question, but also took it seriously.

These good people were paid to play a part in a fabricated world. But, that didn't make the stressors they experienced every day any less real. I believed Brian, for example, when he described how demanding some customers could be. And there was a lot to Joanne's comment about not obsessing about the open purse. I've been at blackjack tables when a player on a losing streak takes it out on a dealer, and that is painful to watch. Joanne dealt with that every day. The poolside waitress, Paula, was very funny, but she shared that a lot of the remarks she received from customers were not so funny at all. And I appreciated the commitment of the Super Cr3w guys to keep it real in an entertainment world filled with a lot of temptations.

These people, more than most I suspect, were susceptible to being shaped by the world around them and the hurtful comments said to them. Allowing that outside shaping is a sure way to lose one's self. Keeping it real for my Vegas friends was all about holding on to their true selves while immersed in a world that pried at the grip. That doesn't answer THE purposeful life question, but it was a pretty good answer for a guy stuck in a fake mid-life crisis.

BFF's!

ON LIFTING

"WHEN WILL THIS TIME END?" That's what seniors are pondering during graduation ceremonies. "Where did the time go?" is what their parents are wondering. It was just yesterday that they were lifting up their now capped-and-gowned babies in the hospital.

Lifting. That's a lot of what parenting is about. I have fond memories of lifting up our children soon after we brought them home from the hospital. On the first starry night I would take each outside and, taking a page from the epic mini-series, *Roots,* would lift that baby to the sky and proclaim, "Behold the only thing greater than yourself!" One of these dramatic moments took place in the middle of a Wisconsin winter, thus my decision to not inform Mrs. Hickey about this particular lift.

Parenting requires a lot of lifting. There are thousands of car seat lifts, shortly followed by lifts into the air upon return from work, lifting and dusting off after bicycle falls and lifting up on shoulders after a fantastic game. Other times it is spirits that need to be lifted, when the team was not made and a beloved grandparent had passed on.

But sometimes the best parenting happens when we don't lift at all. There is a wonderful priest in Seattle who, at every Baptism, advises that there are only two ways to parent: One way is to clear a path for your child to walk through and the other is to give the time, patience and skills that allow the child to learn how to clear the path on his or her own. I've seen both approaches during my years working in high schools, and the difference in outcomes is stark come graduation time. The latter nurtures a healthy, balanced person; the former doesn't.

Whenever I've felt tempted to lift our kids when it would be best that I not, I've thought about an image I carry from my childhood. One of my sisters, Robin, suffered from cerebral palsy and she fell down a lot. I recall a time when, while playing in our yard, Robin fell very hard. Right after she hit the ground I looked to our mother, who had been at the screen door watching us while we played. She pushed the door open, appeared to be stepping out, and then pulled back behind the door. My mother had a pained expression on her face as she watched

Robin lift herself up.

At the time I had some understanding of what was going on, but I now have a much better appreciation of that moment as a parent myself. Our kids will and do struggle at times while they are growing up. When they struggle, even to the point of hurting, our natural desire is to lift them up and make everything better. But constantly doing so – while maybe making the parent feel better – does little to help prepare the child to live better.

Even so, knowing that sometimes the best lifting is when we don't doesn't make things easier. My mother's expression is all the proof I'll ever need that parenting is just really hard at times. But I also know that Robin picked herself up with increasing strength as she grew up. My mom's hands were always at the ready, even when she wisely chose to not use them.

When to lift and when to not? There's no handbook for that. I suppose it just comes down to how best to love the child in the moment when the question is encountered.

Which brings me – without a hint of transition – to the Ascension. There is a Christian tradition that Jesus ascended into heaven after his resurrection, a tradition that I have to admit has carried little meaning for me throughout most of my life. The Crucifixion and Resurrection? Loads of meaning. Jesus elevating himself into the air like a kind of holy hovercraft? Not so much. That all changed a few years ago when I heard the story of a friend who had cancer as a young man.

We all would be tremendously upset and concerned for our health upon hearing from a doctor that we had cancer. So was this young man, at first. Almost immediately after hearing the diagnosis, his mind turned to a more anxious, fear-filled thought: "How am I going to tell my dad?"

His father was stern and demanding, a big man accustomed to getting his way. The young man thought himself to be a failure in his father's eyes. He wasn't going into the family's business, he was going into the Jesuits. The young man perceived this – and other decisions he had made – to have been disappointments to his father. He dreaded his father's reaction to the news of his cancer, as if this too would be seen as a failure.

But the young man mustered up the courage to visit his father in his office and then broke the news. He waited for his father's words. Nothing. This was worse than he had thought it would be.

Then the father looked at his son and walked over to him. He grabbed his boy in his powerful arms and just held him and held him. Then the son realized that his father had slowly lifted him off his feet. And the father just held him there.

The Ascension isn't about Jesus propelling himself up to heaven. It's about a father lifting him there. That's the kind of lifting good parents do.

ON THE COLLEGE DROP-OFF

I KEEP ACORNS in my coat pockets. It's a habit that reminds me of visits to parks when our kids were little. They loved sneaking acorns into my pockets and then running away laughing as if they had pulled off some grand caper. I remember one time when all this was going on and I caught the eye of an older gentleman as he walked by. "Enjoy it while you can," he said. "This time passes fast."

It has. A truth punctuated by our first college drop off. This was certainly a big moment for our daughter, one that could only have been eclipsed, I imagine, by the even bigger moment when I gave her my highly anticipated and much practiced, "Dad's Wisdom for College" talk.

A college drop off veteran had told me that it is best to not impart this wisdom at the actual drop off moment. (Something about the difficulty of stringing words into sentences.) So I gave my advice a few days before we drove her to college. And, knowing that such talks trigger a flight response in the daughter, I found the perfect setting: A trip to the grocery store, doors locked and car in motion.

Introverts draw energy from solitude. Extroverts draw it from company. Know who you are, and find your balance.

Dads are awesome; boys are not. Always do what Dad would think is right. Never do what a boy thinks is right.

Do something physical every day. It doesn't detract from studies; it enhances them.

The single most stupid thing done in college is almost always done while drunk. And, while getting high on marijuana may not necessarily lead to doing stupid things, it will lead to not doing much of anything. Don't be stupid.

God has been a friend in your life every day, whether you've known it or not. Bring your friend to college with you, and spend time with your friend every day.

You will never really leave your home.

It's hard to say what the daughter took from these pearls, especially with all the other messages, often mixed, that young people hear as they prepare to head off for college: Explore and find yourself, but not at the expense of earning a marketable degree. Meet new people and take risks, just be ever mindful of all those sexual assaults on campus. Become a lover of learning for learning's sake without worrying about grades, though they may decide your future.

There's no doubt that going to college and starting life is harder on young people today than it used to be. It's a job that starts well before senior year in high school. The job continues at the drop off, which is no longer a perfunctory exercise. There are days of orientation – talks, dinners and sharing of feelings.

And that's just for the parents. Heck, the president of my daughter's college even gave out his personal phone number to parents just in case we needed to call him in the middle of the night. (I do the same thing with parents at my high school, but this guy apparently uses his real number.) I've never felt so nurtured – or exhausted.

I have a good idea what my parents' generation would have thought of all of this nurturing. When my folks drove me from Kalamazoo to Milwaukee for my freshman year, we had one stop along the way (Mars Cheese Castle in Kenosha) and, upon arrival at Marquette, went straight to my dorm room where we quickly deposited the contents of my one suitcase. Mom gave me a hug, dad a handshake, we all commented on the odor from the local pig rendering factory, and then they were gone. Oh sure, I had an orientation. It was given that very night, courtesy of two sailors who tried to mug me while walking back to my dorm. I ran away and hid in a dumpster.

Yes, a lot has changed. But one thing hasn't. That actual leaving moment is just really hard. We followed a friend's sound advice, "Walk away and don't look back." Right before we walked away, the daughter slipped an acorn into my hand. I'm glad I had already said all that I wanted to say. I couldn't talk anymore.

IGNATIAN EXAMEN

What am I *grateful* for today?

When have I felt comforted, uplifted by *God's presence*?

When have I felt s*eparated from God*, actions and thoughts for which I am sorry?

Should I *seek forgiveness* from anyone – including God – for failing to be the person God is calling me to be?

Finally, I ask for the *grace I need*, especially the desire to see more clearly God's presence in my life.

~Amen

NOTES

On Living Small Days

1. *No Exit*, play, 1944 by Jean-Paul Sartre (1905-1980).
2. "Evening," poem from Early Notebooks, 1894 – 97 by G.K. Chesterton (1874-1936).
3. References to *The Spiritual Exercises of St. Ignatius* are generally taken from the Louis J. Puhl SJ translation, originally published by the Newman Press in 1951 and subsequently published by Loyola University Press.
4. St. Ignatius detailed how the Examen should be prayed in *The Spiritual Exercises,* Annotation #43. There are, however, many variations of the original Examen, including the one included in these Notes. See also an excellent online Examen provided as a joint effort of the Irish Jesuits and Loyola Press at www.sacredspace.ie/daily-prayer. Ignatius told the early Jesuits that the daily Examen should never be skipped, and it remains a central component of Ignatian spirituality to this day.

On Finding Your Posts

1. "Indifference" is referenced in SE #179. "The First Principle and Foundation" can be found in SE #23, though the paraphrasing in this chapter is attributed to David L. Fleming SJ.
2. From *Thoughts in Solitude,* book, 1956 by the Trappist monk, Thomas Merton (1915-1968).

On Grad Tidings

1. From Who Are We?, cassette, 1992 by Henri J.M. Nouwen (1932-1996), Ave Maria Press, Notre Dame, Indiana.
2. Jerome Nadal SJ (1507-1580), an early companion and vicar for St. Ignatius of Loyola. Nadal explained Ignatius's teachings and propagated the Society's Constitutions while visiting Ignatian communities across Europe. Also attributed to St. Ignatius of Loyola (1491-1556).

On the Places You Won't Go

1. From "The Candy Man Can," song, 1971 written by Leslie Bricusse (Born 1931) and Anthony Newley (1931-1999) and sung by Aubrey Woods (1928-2013) in the film, *Willy Wonka & the Chocolate Factory,* 1971. Also appearing on *Sammy Davis Jr. Now,* 1972 by Sammy Davis Jr. (1925-1990).
2. The story of Brother Rodriguez SJ can be found in many sources, including *The Jesuit Guide to (Almost) Everything,* book by James Martin SJ (born 1960), HarperCollins Publishing, 2010.
3. From *Oh, The Places You'll Go!,* book, 1990 by Dr. Seuss or Theodor Seuss Geisel (1904-1991).

On Disordered Attachments
1. Scripture passages such as this one in Mark 10:25 are generally taken from The New American Bible.
2. *Fight Club*, film, 1999.
3. While the shopping quotation is often attributed to Gloria Vanderbilt, it also appears to be true that a number of very rich people have said it at one time or another.
4. Kearney and Howard conversation from *Abraham Lincoln: The Prairie Years and The War Years*, book, 1926 and 1939 by Carl Sandburg (1878 –1967).
5. From *The Great Divorce*, book, 1946 by C.S. Lewis, HarperCollins Publishing.

On Technology
1. From *Walden or Life in the Woods*, book, 1854 by Henry David Thoreau (1817-1862).

On Exercise
1. "The Fuse," song by Jackson Browne from *The Pretender*, 1976.
2. "Lose Yourself," song, 2002 by Eminem (born 1972) from the film, *8 Mile*, 2002.

On Discernment
1. *A Man for all Seasons*, play, 1960, movie, 1966 by Robert Bolt (1925-1995).

On Splitting the Posts
1. Wayne Douglas Gretzky, (born 1961), Canadian former professional ice hockey player and former head coach.

On Abundant Living
1. The Nelson Mandela exhortation to his countrymen was drawn from *A Return to Love: Reflections on the Principles of a Course in Miracles*, book, 1992 by Marianne Williamson.
2. *Being and Nothingness*, essay, 1943 by Jean-Paul Sartre (1905-1980).

On Parental Guilt
1. "Cat's in the Cradle," song, 1974 by Harry Chapin (1942-1981).

On Formation
1. *The Andy Griffith Show*, television show on CBS, 1960 – 1968.
2. *Willy Wonka & the Chocolate Factory*, film, 1971.
3. "God taught me as a teacher would teach a student" is paraphrased from the *Autobiography of St. Ignatius*.

4. Picture taken from Combat Medic Graduation Ceremony, US Army, at Ft. Sam Houston, Texas, October, 2016. Pvt. Edward Hickey is situated in the middle.

On Friendship

1. From *Heauton Timorumenos,* play, 170 – 160 BC by Publius Terentius Afer or Terence (195/185 – c. 159 BC).
2. The "raucous laughter" described in an office meeting attended by Ignatius Loyola was documented by his secretary and de facto biographer, Juan de Polanco SJ.
3. St. Teresa of Avila (1515 – 1582).
4. "We are not human beings having a spiritual experience; we are spiritual beings having a human experience" is an attribution to Pierre Teilhard de Chardin SJ that can be found in *The Joy of Kindness,* 1993 by Robert J. Furey, p. 138.

On Dogmatism

1. *The Cost of Discipleship,* book, 1937 by Dietrich Bonhoeffer (1906-1945).

On Goodness

1. "Bonum est diffusuvum sui," *Summa Theologica,* by St. Thomas Aquinas (1265-1274). The English translation used here provided by Fr. Paul Fitterer SJ, 2015.
2. The story of the freshman is adapted from homilies given by Fr. Gordon Douglas, primarily at Bishop Blanchet High School, at various times between 1999-2007. Fr. Doug's rich treasure of spiritual stories may be found in his book, *Hey, Father,* available for purchase at a reasonable price on Amazon.

On God

1. "Jesus Visits Tim Tebow and The Denver Broncos," *Saturday Night Live* Season 37, television show on NBC, 2011.
2. St. Ignatius included the *Anima Christi* in the Spiritual Exercises and, therefore, it is closely associated with him and the Jesuits. It is possible, however, that an unknown author composed this prayer before the time of Ignatius.
3. The Henri Nouwen quotation is taken from his *Life of the Beloved,* Crossroad, 1992.

On Making Mistakes

1. *Shawshank Redemption,* film, 1994 by Frank Darabont, adapted from "Rita Hayworth and Shawshank Redemption," novelette, 1982 by Stephen King.

On Staying Human

1. The renowned education theorist, Haim G. Ginott, may have been the recipient of the "suspicious of education" admonition and he, in turn, made its wisdom known to the world.
2. Rumi (1207 –1273).

On the Francis Effect

1. The commandment to love thy neighbor is prominent in the synoptic gospels.
2. The infamous hedge fund manager referenced is Martin Shkreli, arrested on fraud charges in 2015.
3. Esther Ballestrino de Careaga's impact on Pope Francis when he was a young man is described in *The Great Reformer,* book by Austen Ivereigh (born 1966), Henry Holt Publishers, 2014, pages 37-38, 144, 150-151.

On Rapturous Living

1. The meme is in widespread circulation on social media and, typical of memes, is uncredited.
2. "Suzanne," poem, 1966 by Leonard Cohen, song, 1966 by Judy Collins (born 1939), and song, 1967 by Leonard Cohen (1934-2016).
3. *The Violent Bear it Away*; this quotation from Matthew 11:12 serves as the title for one of the best and most jarring of works by Flannery O'Connor (1925-1964).
4. *The Chronicles of Narnia,* book series, 1950 -1956 by C. S. Lewis (1898-1963). *The Chronicles of Narnia* has been adapted several times, complete or in part, for radio, television, the stage, and film.

On Judging

1. The Ignatian maxim is a paraphrase from the Presupposition in the Spiritual Exercises, #22.
2. *To Kill a Mockingbird,* book, 1960 by Harper Lee (1926-2016).

On Lifting

1. From *Roots: The Saga of an American Family,* book, 1976, Roots, television series on ABC, 1977 by Alex Haley (1920 – 1992).

ACKNOWLEDGEMENTS

Have you ever been invited to attend a gathering in someone's basement to watch a three-hour family vacation slideshow? If so, you will appreciate the trapped feeling some poor souls must have felt when I asked them to help me with this book. Yet, they overcame their flight response and graciously accepted. I am so grateful that they did.

First, I want to thank a generous benefactor who encouraged me to pursue this project and paid for a substantial portion of the printing costs. Proofreading and editing credit go to the sharp eyes and wordsmithing skills of Alice Evans, Shannon Hendricks, Hannah Hickey, Terry Hickey, Frank Majka SJ, Mike Quillin, and Jen Russell. Sheree Fisher researched publishing criteria and carefully prepared the Notes section. Ben Mawhinney brought his fantastic artistic lens to the photographs. Kathy Mathes, graphic designer extraordinaire, pulled it all together into this beautiful book. Finally, the considerate professionals at Nikko Media generously shared their expertise in the printing process.

A couple of months after I had finished the essays I read them again and listened. I heard four distinct voices, all from mentors whose presence and words have sunk deep within me over the years. Their imprint surfaces in many of the essays:

Fr. Frank Majka SJ, my spiritual mentor from Marquette High days, is usually the "wise Jesuit" who is referenced in these pages. No one joins spirituality to life in conversation and writing as well as Frank. I wholeheartedly recommend his blog, *The Bridge,* at www.FrankMajka.com.

The second voice I recognized in the essays belongs to our pastor at Our Lady of the Lake, Seattle. Every week for the past 12 years, Fr. Tim Clark, our monk-priest, has broken open the wisdom of the gospel and love of the Eucharist to our family.

Many of the thoughts I have on working as an administrator

and being a father originated in the words and example of another Milwaukee mentor, Greg Meuler. I could not have found a better role model for either, especially the dad one.

Fourth, and finally, when patience and generosity can be heard in these pages, attribute that voice to my loving wife and best friend, Terry.